Trumpeter's Tale
The Story of
Young Louis Armstrong

by JEANETTE EATON

Illustrated by ELTON C. FAX

New York · WILLIAM MORROW & COMPANY · *1955*

To Paul Nordoff

Composer, musician, and
friend of all creative artists

3 6 5 3

Contents

TRUMPETER'S TALE

1. *The Little Dipper*

"No! Wait! Dat ain't right. Sing it softer 'n' slower!"

In an open plot behind a row of decrepit wooden houses three boys, seated on a pile of cinders, stared at their critic. As he stood in front of them, thin and ragged, with arms waving, he looked like a small scarecrow. But his flashing eyes held the intense concentration of a maestro at rehearsal.

"Whatsa matter, Dipper?" demanded one of the boys, whose hands were poised over an empty wooden box. "Thought we had to play and sing loud to make folks listen."

"Sho!" The serious face of the conductor broke into a grin that showed a mouthful of gleaming white teeth. The size of that mouth had already given the boy the nickname of Dipper. "Dat's right to start wit'," he said. "But not for 'Swanee River.' Dis is a sorrowin' song. De music mus' be soft an' slow."

Three heads nodded assent. Softly two sticks tapped the box. The conductor hummed the notes of a chord. Beating time with one hand, he beckoned one of the boys to stand beside him. Then, to the accompaniment of the drum, the quartet sang in clear treble Stephen Foster's famous lament.

At the last note, the third boy sprang up from the cinders. "Dat sure is pretty, Dipper! Bet dey'll throw us han'fuls of pennies for dat song!"

The Dipper's pleased grin faded suddenly. From the tower of the cathedral in a far section of the town floated the chime of bells. "Hear dat?" he cried. "Dat's six o'clock! Ef I don' git my papers, I'll lose my beat." He faced his companions sternly. "Now you-all meet me right here tomorrow aft'-noon. And mind ya don' tell nobody what we're aimin' to do. Maybe somebody'd stop us if dey finds out."

"Hey!" yelled the drummer. "Don't we practice our tricks tomorrow, too?"

"We sure do," the Dipper bellowed over his shoulder as he scampered off.

Ten minutes later he was on the corner of a busy street with a bundle of evening papers under his arm. Without a pause he called his wares. "Paper, suh? *States* here! *Item* here! All about how de bank in New Yawk gone bust!"

Usually the boy's lusty shout brought smiles to the faces of the customers. But this evening men hurrying home from offices snatched up the newspapers as if something serious had happened. The Dipper's curiosity, however, was limited to the number of pennies he was dropping into his pocket. He knew from past headlines that New York was a big city up north, but he had no particular interest in what went on there.

New York meant nothing to a boy who knew only certain portions of his own town. A forlorn section of New Orleans was his whole world. Most of the time he lived with his mother and sister. At stated intervals he stayed with his grandmother, many blocks away. It was pleasant there. Yet he was always glad to get back to his mother's crowded room on Perdido Street near such landmarks as the Parish Prison, the huge dance hall on the corner, and Matranga's saloon, from whose open door floated the strains of ragtime thumped on a tinny piano. The Fisk School, where the boy was learning to read, write, and count, was almost halfway between his two homes.

The Dipper ran home that night through narrow streets dotted with hissing arc lights at each corner. His heart thumped with pride. Bouncing up the rickety outside stairway to his mother's room, he burst in, shouting, "Ma! I done sold out every paper! Look!"

Bang on the table under a kerosene lamp went a heap of pennies. A wispy little girl sprang up from a corner of the room with a cry of congratulation. A woman at the stove turned to smile upon the merchant prince arriving with gifts.

"Why, Louis Armstrong," she exclaimed in a warm contralto, "I declare you's one right smart boy."

As she brought him a plate heaped with red beans and greens, she said, "Now, honey, you set down and eat. An' here—" she counted out ten pennies from the copper pile—"you jes' keep dis much yo'se'f. You done earned it."

Louis Armstrong was twelve years and six months old that January night. He had been born on the Fourth of July, 1900, in the worst slum of New Orleans. When he was five years old, his father left the family, got a divorce, and remarried. Then his mother, who had found an excellent place to work, moved to better quarters near the corner of Liberty and Perdido Streets.

Because she was away all day at work, she left Louis and his younger sister in the care of their grandmother. The little girl was called Mamma

Lucy because of her kind and gentle ways. She was too mild and good to be much trouble. But Louis, full of life and curiosity, was very often in mischief.

This was inevitable. New Orleans, like most Southern cities, applied the white man's principle of segregation very strictly. There was no awakened social conscience to combat prejudice. Colored people, for whom only menial jobs were available, could afford nothing but the cheapest lodgings, in certain sections of the city to which they were restricted. No projects existed to provide decent housing for families or playgrounds for children. So Louis and his friends had to play in cluttered back yards or foul streets. Of course, with no realization of injustice, they had jolly times at their games.

Louis was naturally a lively boy. He was always willing to be quiet, however, when he could persuade his great-grandmother to tell stories of her girlhood in New Orleans. The old lady lived at his grandmother's house, and whenever she shook off her feebleness to tell stories she could count on two absorbed listeners. From her seat in a creaky rocking chair on the narrow porch, she glanced down at the two children seated on the floor listening in rapt attention.

Louis learned that when his great-grandmother was a girl more people in New Orleans spoke French than English. She told about the wonderful old houses, with balconies framed in lacy iron grillwork, which had been built when the Spanish owned Louisiana. The finest houses, set back from the street in gardens, were built like hollow squares, enclosing paved courts called patios, filled with trees and flower beds, with great tubs of camellias and giant ferns. From such homes lovely ladies stepped daintily into carriages that would carry them to parties or to the opera or to Mass at the cathedral on Sunday.

"How come you see all dat?" Louis asked wonderingly the first time he heard these marvels described. "I never seen dem houses and ladies like dat."

His great-grandmother sighed. "T'ings mighty different now in New Orleans, specially for black folks. Slaves mos'ly had a good time den. My master and missie was good to me. I learned to wait at parties in de big house, and I saw fine gent'men and ladies real close."

Puzzled, the boy gazed up at the brown face, dry and wrinkled like a withered russet apple. "Where'd you live, Granny?"

"Why, in de slave quarters 'longside de house. Sometimes a lot of families was in dere. We had a right sociable time. And on Sundays—oh, lawsie, in Congo Square! How we did turn out in our bes' calicos and ribbons! We'd dance de bamboula and de conjai till we didn't have no more breath left."

"Dance, Granny?" Louis exclaimed. "What did dey play for dancin'?"

"Oh, dere was drums and horns. One man would jingle bells and another made music with a key scrapin' along a cow horn. But de drums was most enough. Beatin' away! Beatin' away! Dat gets in de blood, boy! It sure does! We'd sing and holler to dat beat and feel like we was flyin'."

Louis sprang up to stamp with delight. "Oh, Granny, wisht you could hear de horns and drums playin' in dat dance hall on de corner. It's hot! De folks go wild. Ragtime, dey calls it. De horn player— I could hear him blow all day and all night and never git tired."

There was a sparkle in the old woman's eyes which belied her severe tone as she said, "Louis Armstrong! You don' mean to say you been to dat dance hall!"

An impish grin answered her. "Most always I stands outside. But one night I sneaks in and sets next de wall. De horn was blowin' de roof off and de people was whirlin' and stampin' and shoutin', and eve'ybody ack like crazy wid dat ol' ragtime. Oh-oh, if I could play de horn like dat!"

Pressed by his great-grandmother's shocked questions, the boy admitted that he had stayed in the dance hall on that occasion until two o'clock in the morning. Then his mother had suddenly appeared, slapped him hard, and yanked him home. After that night he had listened to the marvelous rhythms from the sidewalk outside.

The talk about music and dancing that afternoon had made Louis forget the strange word heard for the first time on his great-grandmother's lips. She had been a slave! The word stuck in the boy's mind and he pondered the meaning of it. Somehow he shrank from a direct question. But one day he asked her if she really had been happier in the old days than afterwards.

After musing a bit, the old woman nodded gravely. "Son, seems to me our people ain't very free yet. Not many of 'em has got learnin'. Lots of 'em is bad and wastes money. White folks don't pay no mind if we ain't got a decent place to live. Dey don't mix wid us nohow." Suddenly she was aware of the hurt bewilderment on the child's face and said quickly, "Never you fear, honey. It won't always be like dis. If you make de mos' of your own self, you might find a way clear to de top."

His less optimistic mother and grandmother preached the gospel of patience. They said it would take ever so long before colored people had a real chance. In the meantime, they must work hard and be good and honest. Louis listened respectfully, but on Perdido Street he saw few grownups practicing these principles. At the imitative stage of childhood, he was bound to copy certain less than admirable adult doings.

One day his great-grandmother caught him making the most of a talent she abhorred. He was squatting on the street near home, absorbed in a dice game with two other small urchins. Louis was just handing over six cents he had lost when a pair of shaky old hands tugged at his collar and a shrill voice commanded him to stop that wickedness and come right home.

Hobbling up the steps, still clutching the collar of the evildoer, she said, "Marie Laveau goin' to voodoo you for sure! Playin' craps! And your good mammy need money so bad. You better make your peace wid Marie Laveau quick!"

With a delighted pounce on this change of subject, Louis asked, "Who dat Marie Laveau, Gran'-mammy? She live roun' here?"

Panting with effort and indignation, the old woman sank into her rocking chair. Solemnly she shook her head at the question. "No, son, she dead now. But she was Voodoo Queen of New Orleans and she ain't lost her power yet, dead or not. She can fix you good for bein' so wicked."

A quavering voice asked what the Queen might do. It appeared that she might cause a naughty boy to break a leg or drown in the river or get lost for good and all. So terrifying was the prophecy that Louis began to howl in despair.

For a few moments his great-grandmother rocked in silence. Then she said, "Now hush! I tell you what we'll do. If you're sorry for shootin' craps, we'll go up to Queen Marie Laveau's tomb in de cemetery and leave her each a dime and say a prayer dat she don' do nothin' to you."

Brightening at once, the sinner confessed that he had won a dime in the dice game before losing six cents and was thus prepared to buy his pardon. The very next Sunday the two set forth. The old burial ground, St. Louis Cemetery, was near beautiful Lake Pontchartrain north of the city. Since that was too far for feeble old legs to walk, the excursion began with the boy's first trolley ride. This was exciting, indeed, but it involved a disappointment. Louis had wanted to sit in the front of the car, but he was firmly dragged to the rear.

"You gotta learn de rules," muttered his great-grandmother. "White folks don't let us sit wid dem. We always has special places in streetcars and trains." When Louis, with puzzled face, asked why, she shook her old head in mild impatience. "Dat's de way it is!" she said with sad finality.

Then, to divert further questions, she launched into the strange history of Marie Laveau. She had been the most powerful Negro in all the region. Even white people feared and honored her. Often beautiful Creole women from the French Quarter asked her for love potions. She lived in the woods near the lake, where an altar was set up for voodoo ceremonies which took place at midnight. Always a big black snake confined in a wooden box was a feature of the occasion. Before the altar a great iron pot was set to boil over a fire and members of the company threw in frogs, toads, small snakes, and turtles. Finally everyone sipped a bit of the brew. Then wild dancing began to the beat of drums. Singing changed to weird cries and the whirl of figures grew faster and wilder. Throughout the fantastic scene Marie Laveau brooded—brooded and danced. If she looked even once directly into the eyes of a man or woman, that individual was sure to be lucky in love.

As he listened in fearful fascination, Louis felt himself taking part in the rites. Moonlight dripped through the dark woods and gleamed on the figures swaying around the boiling cauldron. Shrieks pierced his ears. Looking back to the night at the dance hall, he saw that the crowd there was gentle and serene by comparison. Before him, lifted in the smoke of the fire near the altar, the Voodoo Queen rose like a terrible genie.

Just at that moment the streetcar stopped and Louis jumped down behind his granny. When they entered the open gates of the cemetery she was suddenly silent. Trudging behind her down the narrow

aisles flanked by huge tombs of stone, the little boy shook with nameless dread. At last they stopped. Without a word, Granny flung out a dramatic arm to point at the monument carved with Marie La-veau's name. He stared in awe. Beneath the name were words, but he could not make them out.

Aware that his great-grandmother was laying a dime upon the narrow ledge of the monument, he fumbled in his pocket. Suppose his dime was lost! Would the Queen rise up out of that stone and kill him with one look? His fingers pinched the coin. Ah! He was safe now. Standing on tiptoe, breathing hard, he laid the offering on the ledge. For an instant his whole self throbbed with a plea for mercy. Then a squirrel's little head appeared over the top of the tomb and bright eyes stared at him. A bird with blue wings flew over his head with a high, sweet cry. He saw that the sun was shining, that his great-grand-mother was smiling, and that the delicate fronds of a pepper tree were waving gaily in the breeze. "She ain't a-goin' to git me drowned or lost!" he shouted.

No creature so filled with joyous relief could stay in a stuffy room that evening. Perdido Street was the only outlet for such a mood. Something was always going on there, and in a vague way Louis knew that wickedness lay behind the excitement. He had learned that in rooms at the rear of saloons men gambled away their wages. Often young fellows in gay waistcoats could be heard boasting of picking pockets on Canal Street.

The boys on Perdido Street were inevitably infected by such germs of corruption. Louis often heard boys of fourteen and fifteen cursing and coarsely commenting on the doings of adults. He saw them snatch bananas and pineapples from peddlers' carts and market stalls. Too deeply affected by his mother's disapproval of such bad behavior to imitate it himself, he sometimes acted as lookout for these older boys. His whistling or singing the chorus of "Dixie" gave warning of danger from the proprietor or even a policeman. As a reward, some bit of stolen fruit would be dropped into his eager hands to be consumed later.

Louis was seated on a doorstep one afternoon enjoying an orange when the shadow of the law fell upon him. The very policeman whose approach he had announced in time to scatter the youthful robbers stopped in front of him.

"Where'd ja git that orange, kid?" he asked. Receiving no answer but a frightened look, he said, "Guess you're one of the Perdido Street gang! Worst gang in town."

For an instant the unfamiliar term puzzled Louis.

Then his "No, I'm not" rang out with all the force of innocence. Strolling off with a shrug, the officer left behind him an exciting impression of the importance achieved by these boys. So they were gangsters! After that disclosure, Louis served as lookout with even more ardor.

Nobody could live in the poverty and congestion of the Third Ward without growing used to violence. In wretched shacks or single rooms where privacy was unknown, sudden furies were apt to explode—a natural result of the frustration and resentment of oppression that most Negroes had learned to conceal. Quarrels begun there or in saloons would finish on the street.

Louis, growing up in this jungle, thought of battles as the natural outcome of disagreement. By the time he was ten years old, he was asserting his own manhood with his fists. When his mother came home to find her son with a bloody nose or a bruised eye, she tearfully begged him not to fight. Sometimes, to keep him away from Perdido Street, she told him to come after school to the house where she worked.

She was serving as cook in a wealthy family. Their home was in the residential section, where flower beds, arching trees, blooming shrubs, and velvety lawns made a lovely panorama of the streets. Often, as soon as school was out, Louis found his way there and slipped through the garden hedge. As a signal, he gave two piercing whistles and waited for the answer. If his mother came to the kitchen window and waved a dish towel, he skipped across the lawn and into the big shining room which was his mother's domain. That was the all-clear signal, meaning that the family had gone out.

"Here, son," his mother would greet him happily, "I save you dis plate from lunch. We had chicken today and I got a hot roll put by."

Delighted with the food, Louis would sit on a kitchen stool and exchange the news of the day with his mother. Sometimes one of the other servants would come into the kitchen and join the chat. If Louis came on a Saturday, he might report a trip to the river with his friends. He had learned to swim as a tiny child and loved nothing so much. Down by the docks, where the freighters and coal barges tied up, there was a sweeping view of the Mississippi. The city was built on a curve of the mighty river as it made its divided way to the Gulf of Mexico.

"Dat ol' river's fun," declared the boy. "Boats steamin' out, boats comin' in. Sailors and barge men talk to us while we swim aroun'. But de bes' is at night. When we's swum enough to git cool, we gits dressed and sits and sings all de songs we know."

His mother laughed and patted his head. "It's a

good sight better dan fightin' and playin' craps."
Then, turning to her fellow worker, the chamber-
maid, she said firmly, "My son's a good boy. He
ain't mean and he wouldn't steal a feather off'n a
chicken. Someday I'm goin' to show him roun' dis
house. He wouldn't touch nothin'."

She was always promising this exhibition. And
one day she was able to keep the promise. When
the boy's shrill whistle announced his arrival at the
hedge of the big house, he received a surprising answer. His mother came out on the kitchen stoop
and called, "Come on in! De folks is away on a trip."
When he reached her side at a lope, she said happily, "We all alone. Even all de other maids is gone.
So I'm goin' to show you all over de mansion."

It was an experience Louis never forgot. Awe-
struck, he tiptoed from the dining room, with its
crystal chandelier and massive silverware on side-
board and tables, through a wide and gracious hallway into the parlor and library. His feet sank into
thick rugs. His amazed glance traveled from rows
of books high as the ceiling to handsome lamps and
ornaments, from tables of shining wood to chairs
and sofas of rich color and inviting softness. Afraid
to touch the polished balustrade, Louis padded up
the stairway behind his mother. Unbelievingly he
stared at huge beds with fringed canopies and into

white-tiled bathrooms where tubs almost big enough for a swim grew out of the walls.

Not until they reached the kitchen did the boy break his breathless silence. "Oh, Mammy, it's wonderful!" he gasped. "I never seen nothin' like dis!"

Watching his radiant face with fond eyes, his mother thought, He ain't envious. He don't ask why white folks have such a house while black folks live in one room on Perdido Street. My Louis jes' takes joy in sump'n' beautiful.

Mrs. Armstrong did not understand at first the thing that became her son's chief joy in his twelfth and thirteenth years. She was not aware that in the scorned slum sections of New Orleans something wonderful was rising above sordidness and violence. Music! A new kind of music!

Just as the spirituals once sprang from the lips of slaves to express their hidden longing for freedom, so these inventions of rhythm and melody burst from the troubled hearts of twentieth-century Negro musicians as expressions of sorrow or means of release. Just as the moving quality of the spirituals captured the appreciation of white listeners throughout the country, so the power and genius of the new music surged over the barriers of prejudice and swept Negro musicians into the hitherto denied white realm. Naturally, it was heard first in the

honky-tonks along Perdido Street, then in the cabarets of Basin Street. Presently a band of colored
musicians was playing these novel arrangements.
And anyone who heard that band spread its fame.
Soon it was hired to play at exclusive clubs and
fashionable dances. At last colored artists had created
something that white people simply had to have.

"What kinda music dis?" Louis asked his pals.

"What on earth are they playing?" he heard people on the street say to one another. Most of those
who heard it, however, did not question it. They
just danced to it, tried to whistle it, and begged for
more.

Some of the strains were sad. Blues, they were
called, because they expressed the suffering of an
oppressed people. Other strains were loud and gay.
Of course, tunes can be either gay or sad, but this
music had a different movement from anything
heard before. It pulsed to rhythms that seemed to
be pulling against one another. The horn or clarinet
took flights of its own, while drum and piano tapped
out a time that didn't match, yet sounded right.
Every few bars came a pause—a pause that somehow
compelled the listener to fill it in with a swing of
the body or tap of the feet. Within a few months
all New Orleans had caught the contagion of this
music and a number of bands were playing it.

Louis Armstrong hung outside doorways and pressed close to windows to hear better. Often he would be reminded of a stevedore's song or a hymn of his great-grandmother's or a peddler's chant. But the way the theme was handled was new and strange. Ragtime was grand. But this music sent shivers down the boy's spine. He thrilled with satisfaction when he heard what people had begun to call it. "Jazz! Dat's it!" he cried. "Dat names it sho nuff. Dis music jes tears you apart and twists you round!"

Louis' response to the new kind of music was instinctive and profound. He could neither judge it nor imagine its import. Indeed, the dark-skinned players themselves had not the slightest inkling of its significance. They knew only the glorious release of creation. Having no studios in which to work, they gathered in deserted cabarets at five in the morning to practice, improvise, and invent new cadences. The famous ragtime player, Jelly Roll Morton, egged them on with fleet fingers running along the piano keys. Yet he did not understand that from now on ragtime would be supplanted. Who, indeed, could have guessed then that from New Orleans and Memphis jazz would sweep to Chicago, west to San Francisco, east to New York; that its basic structure was to inspire the creators of light music throughout the United States and influence the most noted composers in both America and Europe?

Louis' share in this upsurge of genius was a tireless effort to follow the beat and catch the minor tones of a blues song. He was thirteen when he organized his own band of minstrels. He had chosen from among the youngsters who sang through the long twilights on the docks by the Mississippi the three with the best voices. Gathered in a back lot, the quartet practiced old familiar tunes. Then Louis, sure that his own enthusiasm was general, taught them the jazz song called "Tiger Rag."

January in the Crescent City close to the Gulf of Mexico is velvety soft. Through violet dusk one night the moon was doing more than the street lamps to illuminate the group of four youngsters as they started out. Two weeks of rehearsals had perfected their performance and at last they were putting it to the test. With canny judgment the Dipper, whose black eyes had been rolling first toward one side of the street and then the other, called a halt before a house on Perdido Street. The open slats of the shutters revealed a group of girls at the bay window. After tipping his cap to them with an engaging grin, the leader whirled to his fellow singers and beat a few measures. Then the mild evening air was shattered by four voices, accompanied by loud thumps upon a wooden box, booming out "There'll Be a Hot Time in the Old Town To-night."

The effect was magical. Shutters flew open. Heads leaned from windows. Figures stepped out of door-ways and a group of strolling sailors and girls stopped to encircle the singers. When the song ended, laughter and applause exploded. As the boys, bowing and smiling, made their way about the audi-ence, coins tumbled into their proffered caps. For half an hour the quartet went through their pro-gram. They did double somersaults, contortions, and buck-and-wing dances. They sang "Tiger Rag" and "Swanee River" and "Mr. Moon, Won't You Shine on Me?"

When the Dipper gave a solo rendition of "Every-body's Gal is My Gal and Your Gal's My Gal Too," coins and laughter pelted him from all sides.

Even in the intoxication of first success, the min-strels kept a lookout for trouble. They were the first to see two policemen, with clubs swinging, ap-pear at a far corner, and they took to their heels just in time. Peering from behind a barricade of ash cans in a nearby alley, they watched the policemen gaze suspiciously down the street. Soon, finding it empty and innocent, the keepers of law and order walked away.

Safe again in the lot behind the shacks, the boys squatted in a circle and dumped all their coins in a central heap. Amid the copper hoard shone many nickels, half a dozen dimes, and even a few quarters. "We rich!" screamed the minstrels, rolling in delight. Then gravely they divided up their earnings.

Jumping up with pockets jingling, Louis Armstrong looked proudly down at his performers. "I done tole you we'd do it!" he said. With an expression of pure joy, he added, "Doggone, wait till my mammy see dis!"

The initial success was followed by others. In darkness or moonlight the boys set forth to sing for pennies. They were often chased by police and almost always reached their homes at a late hour, bedraggled and exhausted. In vain Louis' mother protested, "Chile, how you gonna keep awake at school when you gits to bed at dis hour?"

The fun of performing, the excitement of eluding the law, the savor of violence and excitement beyond the open doors on Perdido Street were not to be given up lightly. Furthermore, Louis was proud to contribute to the household purse these new additions to his earnings from selling papers.

One evening in the late spring Louis joined his three fellow singers with an intensely dramatic air.

"Know where we goin' tonight?" he asked in the low tone of conspiracy. "We goin' to de Distric' to try our luck."

No wonder three pairs of eyes fixed him incredulously. That part of New Orleans, also called Storyville, was forbidden ground for Negroes. Basin Street, the most notorious spot in the District, regarded its own type of lawlessness and evil as far superior to what went on in dark-hued Perdido Street. Police had been well paid by saloonkeepers to keep Negroes out of Storyville and to wink at everything else. For some time Jelly Roll Morton had been the only colored man accepted on Basin Street. Lately, however, Negro bands had become a regular feature of cabaret entertainment. For jazz had been created and was played only by colored artists.

Louis looked mischievously at his thunderstruck companions. "Come on!" he urged. "Big dough's waitin' for us!"

Tense with resolution, the minstrels made their daring way along forbidden streets. It was still too early in the evening for the bands to be filling the air with syncopation. The four singers offered a welcome diversion. Audiences gathered quickly and, with the recklessness typical of honky-tonk patrons,

flung money at the entertainers. Up and down the
narrow streets of Storyville they tap-danced, sang,
and entertained.

As Louis finished his personal interpretation of
"Tiger Rag" he heard a woman's hoarse voice call
out, "Come here, boy!" He stepped to a dimly
lighted doorway. With popping eyes he watched a
red-haired woman in a tawdry evening dress pull

out a huge roll of bills. Peeling off two dollars, she handed them to the Dipper. "That's my favorite song, kid," she said, unsmiling, "and you sang it fine."

A few evenings after this incident the inevitable happened. From the doorway of a saloon a policeman strode out, grabbed two boys by the collar, kicked the other two, and roared a command to get out of the District and never come back. Like four bats the intruders flew off. Once back in Perdido Street, they tumbled into a candy store to celebrate their escape with booty by ordering ice cream and pralines.

With impudent defiance of police injunctions, the minstrels invaded Storyville time after time. To pick up several dollars each was worth the risk, and they were never captured again. One night, however, the boys met a new threat. Somewhat depressed by a sudden rainstorm which had spoiled their performances and reduced their profits, they hurried back to their own territory. Hardly had they entered the Third Ward when six tall youths rushed from an alley to surround them.

"Come on, kids!" commanded the biggest fellow. "Hand over ya cash! Quick now or we'll beat the life outa ya!"

They were members of the Perdido Street gang,

grown to manhood and become enemies. In vain
the minstrels whimpered and protested. A few twists
of their arms and loud threats of betrayal to the
police forced them to yield their pitiful earnings.

Louis regarded the leader in fury. "It ain't fair!
I used to scout for ya an' now ya turn an' rob me!"

"Aw, ya got paid, didn' ya?" The young man
growled the retort, but his expression had changed.
Sheepishly he held out a quarter. "Well, take dis
back and we'll call it quits."

From then on the quartet had to watch out for
the gang as well as for the police. Actually, it added
an extra thrill to the nights' adventures. Summer
and autumn passed quickly and jubilantly for Louis.
He swam in the river; he listened to a new jazz band
at the dance hall near his home, where a wonderful
trumpeter was the sensation of the town. Suddenly
in mid-December he found himself deep in plans
for New Year's Eve. Youngsters liked this celebration even better than Mardi Gras, because everybody joined in the fun and they took active part.
All the boys of Louis' age began discussing the tricks
they were planning for New Year's Eve and Louis
applauded them all. He himself did not reveal the
special stunt he had in mind.

When he first opened his eyes on the morning of

December 31, 1913, Louis chuckled with glee over his secret. What a sensation he would make!

And he did. But not as he had planned. In a single instant of that New Year's Eve the whole course of Louis Armstrong's life was changed.

2.

Satchmo

It was at his mother's home that the holiday began for Louis. Sleeping late, he dawdled luxuriously over the breakfast his sister cooked for him. It was almost noon when an explosion of firecrackers down in the street made Louis jump up from the table. He snatched up a package and dashed out. In another moment he was in the middle of the crowd of youngsters gathered on the sidewalk. The exciting odor of smoke, the bang and splutter of firecrackers, and the sharp smash of torpedoes made the street seem like a battlefield.

In a twinkling Louis unwrapped his package, lighted the fuse of a giant cracker, and flung it into the middle of the street. From that moment he was in the center of action. Noise, laughter, mischief, and merriment filled the afternoon hours. Grown-ups and children, white and colored, set off crackers, popped toy pistols, blew penny horns, and paraded in crazy costumes. The whole ward, usually so

41

sleepy in the daytime, was one hilarious carnival.

As light faded into dusk, Louis rounded up his three singers. "We gotta start our p'formance," he commanded, "befo' it gits late."

"Dat's right," agreed the drummer. "I got my drum box right over here. But, Dipper, we ought to have sump'n' to make a real noise for startin' off. Ain't you got no mo' cannon crackers left?"

Louis' black eyes sparkled and his teeth gleamed in a triumphant grin. Now at last was the moment for his big surprise. "Jes' you-all wait a minute!" He dashed off and raced back to the house.

Meanwhile, his troupe of three had sauntered on. They were almost at the corner of Perdido and Rampart Streets when Louis caught up with them. Before they could yell their amazement at the huge object he was carrying, he tipped it skyward and pulled the trigger. The tremendous bang that followed dwarfed all other sounds for half a block. Then came cheers from his friends and laughter from bystanders. Louis noticed with triumph that several members of the Perdido Street gang were gazing at him enviously.

"Look at that!" cried one man. "The kid's gun is bigger than he is!"

"Whar'd you git dat, Dipper?" screamed the minstrels in chorus.

Louis fondled his weapon with pride. "It's my daddy's old thirty-eight. Mammy hid it away, but I found it sho' nuff."

"You could kill a dozen men wid dat," declared the drummer fearfully.

"Naw," laughed Louis. "It's loaded wid blanks. Come on now. Let's get goin'. We'll sing 'Mister Moon.'"

As the last note died away amid applause and a shower of pennies, a small white boy came swaggering down the sidewalk. He was snapping away with a little cap pistol.

"Look at him!" sniffed Louis. "I'll show him what a real gun can do." Aiming high, he fired twice.

The little boy, quite unaware of anything but his own gun, was almost facing Louis when the blast went off. Stopping dead, he began to scream with terror. Louis, dumbfounded at this unexpected reaction, stepped forward to reassure him.

At that instant a heavy hand fell on his shoulder. A harsh voice cried, "Shooting at a white boy, are you? You come along with me!"

Twisting about, Louis saw a policeman towering over him. In vain he babbled that he had shot into the air, with blank cartridges. In vain his three friends shouted, "Mister, he didn't do nothin'!"

Impelled by a powerful grip, Louis was hustled

down the street and shoved into the back of a big steel box on wheels. With a bang of the rear door, darkness closed in. And now Louis realized what was happening. Often he had seen this wagon carry off drunks and cutthroats from Perdido Street. "De Black Maria! Dey's takin' me to jail!" he moaned.

Shock and anxiety blurred the details of the next hour. Later he remembered the wagon's jolting along the street with its bells ringing. It stopped shortly and then he was mounting steps beside the policeman. Near the entrance of the building a man in a shabby uniform exchanged comments with the policeman. Next, Louis found himself shoved into a sort of cage with only a cot inside. He stood shivering in the lonely dark. What was going to happen to him? The sign above the doorway—*Detention Home*—had told him where he was, and he had heard the guard say, "Guess the judge will hear the kid's case in the morning." Then what, he asked himself in dread. Even when he stretched out on the cot, he could not sleep. Out of each doze he would start up at the sound of groans and curses from nearby cages. A blend of horrid smells piercing the odor of disinfectant almost stopped his breathing. How had such a fate befallen him?

Never had he been more thankful to see morning light at last. There was a long wait, however, before anything happened. First, a tray with food was shoved into his cage. Then, after he had been heartened by the bun and the cup of milk, the man in uniform escorted him into a big, dim room. Several youths and girls, both colored and white, sat on benches in front of a platform on which a big table was perched. Behind it, facing the room, sat a grave, quiet middle-aged man. One by one, each culprit was summoned by a policeman to stand beside the table while the officer read out his or her misdeeds in a loud voice. At last it was Louis' turn.

"Judge Wilson," said the policeman sternly, "here is one of the worst hoodlums in the Perdido Street gang. He was caught red-handed, shooting at a little white boy. This was the weapon, sir." He held aloft the confiscated gun.

"It ain't so!" bawled Louis. "Dey was blank cartridges and I was aimin' high. I was *not* shootin' at him!"

Looking straight at him with keen blue eyes, the judge asked in a low tone, "What is your name and how old are you?" After hearing the choked-out answers, he said, "Well, Louis Armstrong, we have a lot of trouble with residents of Perdido Street, young and old. Even if you didn't shoot to hurt the white boy, you were risking other people's safety by firing that gun. A boy of thirteen ought to have more sense. You are going to be taught how to behave where I am going to send you. Here, Officer"—the judge wrote out a slip—"have this boy taken to the Colored Waifs' Home."

Again a trip in the wagon, a longer one than before. Again Louis was told to get out and hurry up a flight of steps. In the hallway of the big building a colored man stepped forward. Through his cloud of terror Louis could hardly make out his face. Would he be kept in another cage or a dark cell?

"Howdy, Mr. Jones," said the driver of the police vehicle. "I've got a fine case for you here—one of them Perdido Street gangsters. Here's Judge Wilson's slip."

During this introduction, Mr. Jones had waved them into a small office. He sat down at a desk, drew out a big book, and entered Louis' half-sobbed replies to questions as to his name, age, address, and schooling.

As soon as the policeman left, Mr. Jones got to his feet and said, "Come upstairs to the dormitory, Louis, and I'll show you your locker. You get yourself thoroughly washed, and then put on the blue jeans and shirt I'll give you."

Louis stared into the big room at the top of the stairs. Some fifty cots, neatly made, stood in two rows down its length. At least it was not a cell! His guide laid a sheet of paper bearing Louis' name upon a cot near the middle of the room.

"This will be your bed," said Mr. Jones. "Here is your locker just behind it. Put those clothes you have on in it. Through that door is the washroom. I'll put your new clothes on your bed. When you're clean and dressed, come down to my office."

The comfort the boy felt at being clean again was immediately blotted out by his interview with Mr. Jones. First Mr. Jones talked about the Perdido Street gang and their crimes, and how shocking it was that Louis at his age had such bad associations. Next came a long list of rules to follow. Finally Louis was warned that he must obey orders instantly or expect severe punishment. Louis' replies were meek and quiet, but they disguised the wild rebellion in his heart. How could he get out of this awful place? There must be some way to escape to freedom!

A bell rang loudly through the hall. Doors opened on each side, and boys in blue jeans came marching in lines toward a central room with wide-open double doors. "It's lunchtime," said Mr. Jones. "I'll take you along to the dining room."

To the man at the entrance Jones said, "Here's a new boy. I guess he'd better sit with the older group."

"All right, I'll attend to him." The speaker's eyes bored into Louis. A firm hand pushed him across the threshold. "Sit on that right-hand bench. And mind you behave yourself!"

Louis slid into place before a smoking plate of stew. He stared at it, feeling that he could not swallow a single mouthful.

The boy opposite him pushed a pitcher of milk and a glass in his direction and said, "Well, happy New Year!"

Glancing up, Louis felt his lips tremble at the sound of the first friendly words he had heard in eighteen hours. Unburdened by a sense of irony, he managed to respond to the greeting with a feeble grin. "What's your name?" he asked.

"Jim Glass. What's yours?"

After telling him, Louis asked fearfully, "Who dat man at de door?"

"Him? One of de teachers—Mr. Peter Davis. Watch out for him, kid. He got a bite like a wolf!"

The terrifying effect of this statement made Louis feel even worse than before. Unable to eat, he looked about the room. What he saw surprised him. The long rows of faces looked cheerful. Subdued talk and giggles made a low murmur through the mild clatter of dishes and cups. Didn't these boys mind being in such a place? Curiosity made him turn back to Jim Glass. "Dey all crooks an' gangsters here?" he inquired.

Jim laughed. "Not me. Not most of 'em. Lots has no homes, like me. My dad and mammy got sick and died. I hadn't no place to go. Course, some of de kids was brought in by de police. How 'bout you?"

Louis choked and nodded his head. He was glad when lunch was over. Forlornly standing by the wall outside the dining room, he watched the boys stroll by twos and threes into the playground. Only curious glances were flicked in his direction as they passed. Used as he was to sociable companionship, he was chilled to the bone by his sense of isolation. When the bell rang, the boys hurried into classrooms. Presently a woman who, he learned later, was Mrs. Jones, wife of the head of the home, told him to go downstairs to Mr. Alexander's carpentry class.

He pushed open the door shyly. In spite of poor lighting, the big room had a cheerful air, filled as it was with the sound of hammers and saws. Louis felt his spirits rising. But when the teacher placed him with a group engaged in making a bookcase and he tried to take part in the work, he was once more made to feel unwelcome. The boys were openly hostile. Eying him suspiciously, they hurled

low-voiced contempt at his efforts. "Dumbbell, dat ain't de way to do it!" "Watch him wid de saw. He t'inks it's a jackknife." Mr. Alexander's kindly help did little to alleviate his misery.

In the arithmetic class, held upstairs, the teacher, Mr. Jones, seemed determined to show up Louis' ignorance. Unreproved, the others laughed loudly at his mistakes. So large grew the lump in his throat that he could hardly speak at all.

Still more desolating was the reading and spelling class taught by Mr. Peter Davis. His hard, reproving eyes frightened Louis and there was good reason for his fear. After class, for no reason he could discover, he was given a whipping. Gritting his teeth, he managed not to cry, even when the teacher said, "We have no use for boys like you and the rest of the Perdido Street gang." In sarcastic tones he told Louis to cure his aches by joining the boys in the garden, where Mr. Alexander was having them prepare a place for growing spring vegetables.

Sipping his soup at supper, Louis thought of the red beans his mother would be cooking. Never in his life had she let him go hungry. And right this minute she would be worrying about him and feeling sad because of his imprisonment. Not a single boy, not even Jim Glass, said a word to him that evening. It was a relief when, in bed at last with lights out, he could smother his face in the unsympathetic pillow and sob out his unhappiness.

Waking next morning was abrupt. Hands were shaking his shoulders. Voices were crying, "Hey, wake up! De bell's done rung!" Sitting up with a start, Louis stared at the boys on each side of his bed. One of them was Jim Glass, who said gruffly, "Hustle, kid! Dey beats you if you're late to breakfas'!"

The long, dimly lighted room was alive with

figures hastily pulling on their clothes. Subdued murmurs filled it. Louis dressed in a twinkling and rushed through his washing in time to join the tail end of the march downstairs.

That day and the days that followed were grim. Twice Mr. Davis gave Louis a beating. The boys treated him like a pariah. Bitter resentment filled his soul. He longed to fight each one of them separately and then make a dash for freedom.

On Sunday the first streak of light crossed his dark sky, for in the afternoon the school band gave a concert and all the boys attended. Louis had heard the blare of practicing now and then and was eager to discover what the performance would be like. He planted himself on the front bench to watch and listen. The band, eighteen strong, consisted of horns, cornets, triangles, and drums. The conductor was Peter Davis. Louis, whose ear was trained to band music, was happily surprised by the snappy pace and clear tones the boys achieved. He knew the credit belonged to the bandmaster, whose authority and enthusiasm were inspiring the players.

Louis stamped and clapped lustily after every number. He had forgotten his wretchedness for this one absorbing hour. But when, at its end, the leader turned to bow, his stern glance fell upon Louis. With a shudder the boy stopped applauding and dropped his eyes. He thought, Bet dat man don't like me to take pleasure in his music. Bet he finds a chance to beat me tomorrow.

The prophecy came true. Again, for no reason that was explained to him, Louis was given another beating. As before, he suffered in silence. Worse than physical pain was the aching sense that this man whom he could admire, with whom he longed to talk about music, hated him. The fact made the dark days darker, loneliness still more bitter.

It was almost impossible for Louis to slip into the groove of discipline. He had never known restraint. He obeyed commands sullenly, but he could not remember all the rules and was forever breaking them. One evening he committed the sin of strolling out after dark into the playground. When Mrs. Jones screamed at him to come right back, he waved his hand to her, meaning that it was all right, he was not going to run away. But Mr. Jones rushed after him, caught him by the collar, dragged him into the office, and beat him with a leather strap.

If he missed his place in line when the bell rang for a meal, he was forced to miss the meal. Yet, in spite of his hatred of all the rules, he did realize that when he obeyed them he received smiles and kind words from Mr. Jones and his wife and from Mr. Alexander.

Moreover, he rather liked gardening and began to take an interest in making or painting some useful object in the carpentry class. His stupefying fear of Mr. Davis made him dread his class, yet he found himself reading and writing with increasing ease. The Waifs' Home would have begun to feel like a school instead of a prison if only the boys had been companionable. True, they had stopped laughing at him in class and calling him a dumbbell, but they still kept their air of watching him suspiciously. He was determined not to show his hurt and anger and to resist his longing to pummel the most offensive snubbers. Stoically he kept to himself.

Then came a day when the ice thawed. It started in the carpentry class when Mr. Alexander gathered the boys around Louis to admire the bench he had made and painted a bright red. And they did. "It's sure slick!" said one. "Dat's a real gay seat!" said another. Louis grinned with satisfaction over his very first success.

"Look at dat fella smile, Mr. Alexander!" crowed Jim Glass. "Why, he got a mouth big as a satchel."

Amid laughter another youngster cried, "Jus' look at Satchel Mouth. Bet he could swallow his own bench."

Louis chuckled delightedly. He was thrilled an hour later on the playground to be drawn into a ball game by the cry, "Come on, Satchamouth! See if you can catch wid ya teeth!" When a member of the band changed the name to Satchmo, Louis approved it heartily. Instinct told him that a nickname meant he was at last included, accepted as one of the group.

Not long after this baptism, Jim Glass openly adopted him as a friend. "Say, Satchmo," he said one afternoon as they left the reading class, "I couldn't see why Mr. Davis hit you today. You was doin' all right. He's mean to you, ain't he? I bet you hate him like a black snake."

"No, I don't!" replied Louis instantly. "Dat Mr. Davis sure knows music. He kin play every instrument in de band. I jes' wish . . ." His voice trailed off.

Jim looked at him curiously. "You's funny, Satchmo. I'd sure hate anybody dat beat me up like dat. Why, you don't do nothin' bad." He whacked Louis on the back. "I think you're as good a fella as we got."

This, indeed, was the salutation of fellowship. From then on Louis Armstrong began to relax and regain his shattered sense of fun. One night when the lights were out in the dormitory and only moonlight streamed through it, Louis was seized by irresistible gaiety. Softly, but in his old clowning way,

he began to sing "Tiger Rag." In spasms of laughter
the other boys rolled on their cots.

At that moment Peter Davis entered the room.
With one stride he was beside the performer's bed.
"So!" he cried, seizing Louis by the arm. "I might
have known it was you stirring up mischief. Get
into bed now and no more tricks!"

As the door closed behind him, Louis leaned
over to Jim's cot. "What you t'ink o' dat?" he whispered. "He jus' tole me to git into bed. Not even
one whack! I sure b'lieved he'd beat de daylights
outa me."

Although he sank back on his pillow in puzzled

relief, Louis did not interpret the incident as marking a change in the teacher's feeling toward him. Every contact with Davis put him tensely on the defensive.

Sitting happily absorbed in supper one evening, he saw Peter Davis come walking through the dining room. With spoon halted in mid-air, the boy watched him fearfully. To his horror, Mr. Davis stopped right beside him. Was he to be dragged away for another punishment? An upsurge of bitterness swept away all the pleasant memories of the last weeks.

But the tone of Mr. Davis' voice was unfamiliar. And the words—no, they couldn't be meant for him. Looking up incredulously, Louis met the eyes which had so often sent shivers down his spine. It was not the stern teacher looking at him, speaking to him, but the bandmaster. Davis was saying with a friendly smile, "How would you like to play in my band?"

Louis could only gasp in amazement. But he leaped to his feet and his eyes were twin lamps of joy.

"Come over to the window, Louis," urged the pleasant voice. "I want to talk to you." And never had the boy obeyed a command so swiftly.

"I've been watching you, Louis," began Davis, "and I've decided you aren't really one of the Perdido Street gang. I happen to know that pennies and pencil boxes and other things get left around that you could have stolen. But you don't steal and you don't pick fights. You don't lie or tell on other boys. It isn't your fault you had to live in a bad neighborhood. So!" He dropped a hand on the boy's shoulder. "Come along now and I'll give you a lesson on the bugle. I think I'll start you on that."

Stepping into the band's practice room was the beginning of a new life for Louis. The moment he lifted the bugle to his lips he felt as if something wonderful was being born in him. Patiently and skillfully Peter Davis showed him the rudiments of bugle blowing, illustrating every point himself. At the end of half an hour he stopped the lesson.

"That's enough for tonight," he said. "I truly believe, Louis, that you have talent. Your breath control is good. We'll have another lesson tomorrow. I think you'll learn fast."

After a few joyous skips down the hall Louis looked back to see his teacher watching him with a smile. The boy's heart gave an extra bound. Him and me's goin' to be frien's, he thought ecstatically.

Louis did indeed learn fast. Within a week he was sounding the bugle calls for meals, classes, and band rehearsals. Every day his tones grew clearer and more accurate. He played taps for bedtime and reveille for rising.

Often Louis lay awake to wonder how all this had happened. It was a true fairy tale. A wand had been waved and at once the Waifs' Home was turned into a castle of delight. The dreadful ogre had become a prince and the hostile inmates of the castle were now friends.

When he had made a really good start as a bugler, Louis had a glorious reward. He was made a member of the band. To qualify for the honor, he had to learn to play the tambourine and the small drum, and his quick mastery of both instruments won praise from the conductor.

But Louis did not desert the bugle. In early summer the Colored Waifs' Home Band was asked to play for a parade in New Orleans. The uniformed boys marched in good form and at their head was Louis, the proud bugler. He had written his mother about his part in the parade and hoped she could watch it. As the band reached Canal Street, Louis gazed at the handsome hotels, banks, and stores with the interest of a foreign visitor. How he had longed to see that street again! But he had never dreamed of doing so in such glory.

As the band neared Perdido Street, Louis cast

swift glances left and right. Could he possibly distinguish his plump mother and little Mamma Lucy among the cheering crowds? Then, during a pause in the music, he heard a piercing scream—"Louis! Louis!" A red handkerchief wildly waved from the sidewalk marked his sister and mother. He waved his cap. At last they were proud of him! This was the great moment of the afternoon.

It was some time after the parade when the most thrilling event in Louis Armstrong's short life took place. After band practice one afternoon Peter Davis asked Louis to stay a few moments. Wonderingly he waited by the window while the bandmaster fussed with something at his table. Suddenly he turned and said, "Louis, I have a present for you." And before the boy's bulging eyes he waved a cornet.

"Mr. Davis!" roared Louis. "You *givin'* me dis?" He held out both hands, palms upward, with an air of receiving something unutterably precious.

"Yes, I'm promoting you," laughed his teacher. "Take care of this cornet. It's yours as long as you stay here. You'll have to work hard to make it do its best."

Then and there the ecstatic boy was given a first lesson in fingering. There was never a more ambitious pupil. He drank up instruction as if he could never get enough and practiced so continuously that before a week had passed he was permitted to play in the band as second cornetist. He was so nervous that Sunday afternoon that he made mistakes, but the conductor indicated by a smiling shake of the head that he understood why. Before he went to bed that night Louis wrote his mother about the wonderful gift, and signed himself, "Your loving cornet-playing son."

The bandmaster's exacting standards were too much for the patience of many of the players, but never for Louis. He enjoyed going over and over a piece to perfect the rhythm or improve the tone. His zest was so contagious that the leader declared the band was playing better than ever before.

No longer did Louis have to struggle with home-sickness. Perdido Street tricks seemed merely child-ish now. That year of 1914, a year filled with tragedy for the world, brought happiness and satisfaction to Louis Armstrong. He responded so wholeheartedly to every responsibility that Davis made him assistant band leader, with a distinctive uniform. When the others donned their blue coats and white trousers, he wore blue trousers and a cream-colored jacket. Such elegance was not wasted on school concerts, of course, but saved for adult audiences.

During the spring of 1915 Mr. Davis often took his band into New Orleans to play for church sociables and club meetings. The members were much excited one week to learn that they had been engaged to entertain a group of people going on an all-day picnic up the Mississippi.

Early in the morning of the day for the picnic Mrs. Jones lined up the band members to inspect their well-pressed uniforms and polished shoes. "Boys, you certainly look fine," she said with motherly pride. "Now try to keep your suits from getting all messed up."

As she spoke, Peter Davis came rushing from the office. "Boys," he said, "I've been called to a meeting of the trustees of the Home. I can't go along with you. Louis!" He turned to him solemnly. "I'm putting you in charge. I trust you to see that everything goes just as it should."

Louis stepped to the head of the line. With a glowing look of pride he said, "Yes, sir, Mr. Davis, you sure can count on me."

Armed with directions for meeting the picnic party, Louis marched off with his band. Not for the world would he show a sign of the nervousness which brought beads of moisture to his forehead. Since the meeting place was near Baton Rouge, the boys had to take a steamboat from New Orleans. Once he had shepherded the band on board, he could relax for a time and enjoy his first long trip

on the mighty Mississippi. From the boat deck he thought the river looked bigger than ever before. Leaning over the rail, he marveled that the pilot could steer so surely against the powerful current.

At Baton Rouge, Louis marshaled the band for landing. Then he formed them in marching order to reach another wharf where the party waited to ferry across to the picnic place. As they came in sight of the crowd, Louis shouted, "Get ready now! 'Stars and Stripes Forever!' One, two, three! Strike up!"

From the waiting crowd handkerchiefs waved and hands clapped. Just as the marching boys reached the wharf, a loud whistle from the ferry urged the party on board. There was a merry jam of moving figures, bumping picnic baskets, laughter and talk. Words of welcome greeted the band members. "Thank you, boys!" "That's great, boys!" "Glad you're with us!"

Across the muddy river the ferryboat landed the passengers on a muddy shore, but a rough road led up to higher ground where open country was bordered by woods. Louis looked eagerly about at the wild magnolias and flowering shrubs glowing in the spring sunshine. Beyond the picnic grounds lay a cypress swamp with a mass of colorful azaleas framed in dark, twisted trees.

Louis grouped his players on a little rise and

opened the program. Solemn and intent, they launched the band's most ambitious piece, an arrangement Mr. Davis had made for them of part of the overture to "Tannhäuser." The listeners were so spellbound that they did not even open the picnic baskets until the last note had died away, drowned in applause. To prove their versatility, the band then played the "St. Louis Blues," a jazz song so recently popular in New Orleans that Louis was startled to hear half the crowd joining in with the words. After that, requests for tunes were shouted from women setting out food and men opening ginger-ale bottles. The band never failed to respond, and after almost an hour of heroic blowing and drumming the call to luncheon was a sound of piercing sweetness to all the boys.

Louis stared at his plate of fried chicken, spoon bread, cold ham, potato pie, and biscuits. Rolling his eyes, he sighed ecstatically. "Ma'am, dis sho' is heaven!" Yet before he touched a bite he made sure all the other boys had been served.

"Now, you musicians, just do as you please!" said the leader of the picnic group. "We're going to take naps, stroll, and laze around. No more music until we board the ferry again to go home. You've given us fine entertainment, boys, so just relax and take it easy now."

After all the plates were empty Louis instructed his charges. "You-all on your own now, fellas. But mind you don't git lost an' lef' behind."

"What you doin' yo'se'f, Satchmo?" someone asked.

"Me? I'm fixin' to take a look at dat ol' cypress swamp."

"Den you's de one to git lost!"

Waving his hand airily, Louis set off. As he reached the edge of the swamp, he pushed aside the delicate curtains of moss hanging from the trees and crept along between moss-covered stones and fallen logs. Everywhere about him ran narrow streams of inky water. All was weirdly still beneath the lofty canopy of interlacing branches. Just in front of his lifted foot a snake swirled its long, heavy body over a log and noiselessly swam away. The fragrance of azaleas growing on tiny islands accented the dank odors of rotting wood. For some time, as Louis made his cautious exploration, he enjoyed the fantastic scene. Then suddenly weariness overcame him and he stretched out on a bed of moss between the knobby knees of a sprawling cypress. The responsibilities of the day slipped from his shoulders. In two minutes he was sound asleep.

With a start of fear he awoke. Was it night? He could hardly see from one tree to another. Had the crowd gone without him? Grasping a low-hung branch, he jerked to his feet. From which direction had he come? He looked this way and that. Tales of men lost for weeks in cypress swamps rushed through his mind. If he missed the ferry, he would never get back to New Orleans that night and then . . . Mr. Davis! He would have failed him!

A faint cry cut through his anguish. Surely it was a boy's shout. Louis scrambled through the twisting paths, stumbling, pulling himself along with the help of drooping branches. And all at once he was out of the blackness. The sun was shining. He caught a glimpse of moving figures. They were still there. At full speed he ran up the slope, then stopped short. Swiftly he assumed a casual grin and a swagger in his walk as he strolled toward the crowd.

"Satchmo!" yelled the bass-horn player. "Whar you been?"

"Just in time, boy!" interrupted a cheerful voice. "We're all ready to start."

A blast from the ferry whistle saved Louis from explanations. He snatched up his cornet from the table where he had left it and strode down the road. Mixed with his grateful relief was a resolve never again to stray from the path of duty. And he kept this resolution during every excursion that summer.

As time went on, Louis found new stimulus from a rival in the band. His name was Kid Rena and he played the cornet too. It became a game with the two to see who could play the loudest and hit the highest note.

The activities of that speeding summer blotted out entirely from Louis' mind the fact that he had been sent to the Colored Waifs' Home as a punishment. He felt much as any boy does about a private school where he is happy. Loyalty to the Home and a will to make good were his unconscious impulses. As a natural result, the faculty of four had become his warm friends. Often Mr. Jones and his wife invited him to their study to share a dish of ice cream or a thick chocolate layer cake. Mr. Davis had finally converted Louis to the idea that reading might actually be fun. Finding that he was a regular patron of the small collection of shabby volumes glorified by the name of school library, Mr. Davis gave him a book of his own.

"I sure like dat story 'bout Huck Finn, Mr. Davis," reported the convert. "But how did dat Mark Twain writer know our ol' Mississippi River like dat? He had every trick—good and bad—of dat river by heart."

"Well, sonny." Davis smiled. "First of all, Mark Twain was brought up in a Mississippi River town.

When he was a young man he became a river pilot of one of the regular steamboats, so he had to learn everything about that big river, every island and shoal. He wrote a book about that, too."

Louis' eyes snapped with interest. "Some day I'd sure like to go up to where the river begins. Say, Mr. Davis, de bes' would be ef I ever could be in a band on one of dem river boats."

"Just you keep on with the cornet, Louis, and maybe you could join such a band."

One morning in early autumn Louis was called from class to Mr. Jones's office. As he stood waiting to find out why, he thought the head of the Home was looking at him in a rather odd way. After a moment he said, "Get your bugle, Louis, and call everyone into the hall. We're going to say good-by to somebody who's leaving us."

At the imperative notes of the bugle, boys hurried out of classes and in from the garden to form ranks for the roll call. Both Mr. Anderson and Mr. Davis came in also.

"What dis all 'bout, Satchmo?" whispered one boy after another. The answer spread through the ranks as wind sweeps through a wheat field. One of the boys was leaving the Home. But who? Wondering eyes rolled from face to face. Shoulders shrugged. Nobody knew.

Mr. Jones came from his office at last. "Well, this is a special occasion," he began. "One of our boys is leaving today. He has worked hard and behaved well. He has shown a marked sense of responsibility for the good of our school. So we have decided to let this boy go back home."

There was a long pause. Again heads turned this way and that, seeking the answer to the mystery.

"I'm sure you'll all be glad when you hear who this boy is," went on Mr. Jones deliberately, "although we'll miss him here. We certainly wish him luck. Louis Armstrong, you are the boy!"

Louis dropped the bugle with a clatter. "Me?" he gasped.

Smiling at his astounded look, Mr. Jones said, "Go up and get your things together, son. You're leaving right away."

Leaving the band! Giving back his cornet! Leaving Mr. Davis and Jim Glass and Kid Rena and his other pals! Dazed with shock, numb with a strange ache in his heart, Louis stumbled upstairs to his locker. Boys crowded around him, looking solemn, looking envious, all trying to joke. As he came down with the bundle of his possessions under his arm, cries rose from below and were echoed from above. "Good-by, Satchmo!" "Don't forgit us, Satchmo!" "Luck, ol' Satchmo!"

Louis' responses were choked-out murmurs and feeble grins. When Mr. Davis stepped from his door to shake hands, Louis dropped his bundle and seized the bandmaster's hand in both his own. "Mr. Davis," he stammered, "I—I—will I ever see you again?"

Assuring his cornetist that he would always be welcome as a visitor, Davis patted him on the back. Louis turned away quickly. He felt split asunder. It was like being expelled. All at once he saw his mother approaching from the end of the hall. A rush of gladness carried him into her outstretched arms. "Mammy," he cried, "it's sure sump'n' to see you again!"

It was good also to walk freely along the old streets on the way home. A lunch of his favorite red beans and rice, cooked only as his mother could prepare them, was nothing less than glorious. Yet that night in the dark Louis took a glance at the future with leaden heart. What now? No more cornet playing, or classes, or excursions. He had to go out and hunt for a job. A groan escaped him. He had been catapulted into manhood.

3. *Reveille*

For two years the struggle was grim for Louis Armstrong. It seemed to him that everybody could get jobs except himself. He did, however, win back his post at the newsstand, selling evening papers. Once again men coming back from work heard Louis, taller now but still very thin, calling at the street corner, *"States* here! *Item* here!"

As he glanced through the papers to select the headlines to call out, Louis began to realize that the war in Europe was truly important. At the Waifs' Home, he had only vaguely realized there was fighting over there, and even now the war across the seas seemed very far away. Yet sales mounted swiftly when he yelled, "Huns sink another ship!" "All about German advance!"

Nevertheless, the money Louis earned by selling papers was far from enough for self-support. He knew he must work during the day to earn money for the board he paid to his mother and for clothes.

Reluctantly he went down to the levee and signed up for employment at the docks as a roustabout, to load and unload cargoes. During the first week he heaved gigantic sacks of bananas and crates of merchandise from the holds of ships to the wharf or onto waiting trucks. He did not have the muscular strength for such heavy work and before a fortnight ended he had strained his back severely. For several days he had to stay in bed, wracked with pain. It was all he could do to stagger out to his paper stand.

"Guess you ain't strong enough for a dock job," said his mother, with a worried look at her son. "Pity you ain't got no skills like 'lectrical work or bein' a bus boy in a restaurant. I ask my folks at de mansion if dere's any work for a smart kid around dem fine places, but dey say ev'y place is overrun wid garden boys and such."

In vain Louis roamed Storyville in search of work. He knew it was no use to try for employment in the Canal Street stores. His forlorn patched clothes and broken-toed shoes would rule him out at once.

After weeks of idleness he was finally hired by a dairy firm. But once more he proved unequal to the hard physical labor. Lifting heavy cans of milk strained his back again and he was forced to quit. During the next period of idleness there was nothing to relieve his misery. He thought with heartache of the protected, regular life of the Waifs' Home and the joy of playing in the band. There seemed no hope that he would ever get back to the music that had meant more to him than anything else. Playing his cornet had made him forget the hardships of his life. Now that release seemed to be gone forever.

Finally he got a job he could keep. It was with a coal merchant who employed several men to sell small lots of coal from mule-drawn wagons. First as helper, than as driver of a cart, Louis covered one section of the Third Ward. "Stove coal, ladies!" he shouted. "Five cents a bucket. Coal here!"

When an answering call came from window or doorway, he climbed down from the cart, filled a

bucket from the wagon, and carried it into the
buyer. His hours were long and the pay was small.
He got up at five in the morning and was on his
route till late in the afternoon, with a few minutes
off at noon to eat the cold lunch he had brought
from home. He worked so faithfully that after a
month or two the coal merchant gave him a raise.
"You're a good salesman, Louis," he said, "and you
seem to get along fine with the mule."

Louis was glad to have even so unrewarding a
job. Now, after paying his board and buying shoes
and clothes, he could afford a little fun once in a
while. Dance halls were his favorite haunts. If he
could no longer make music himself, at least he
could listen to it. It was easy to persuade his partners
to teach him to dance the Charleston and a ludicrous
step called the shimmy that was just becoming the
vogue. He liked dancing and ragtime piano playing,
but his real devotion was given to the jazz bands.

No one knew better than he what exciting progress jazz was making. New tunes or arrangements
were introduced daily. The nearby dance hall had
a trumpeter who could improvise all sorts of musical decorations for a melody. Everywhere these days
Louis heard extravagant praise of another trumpeter, named Joe Oliver, who was playing with
Kid Ory's band at the largest cabaret in Storyville.

One Sunday afternoon Louis went to the big recreation park where Ory's band was going to play. Pushing up as close to the platform as possible, he fixed his eyes at once on the tall, muscular man who played the trumpet. From the first note of Joe Oliver's solo, Louis was entranced. With rapt attention he noted Oliver's originality in phrasing and marveled at the pure perfection of his tone. Ah, this was joy! It was sorrow, too. For the first time in his life Louis was pierced with envy. Joe Oliver did not have to heave coal for a living. He had the finest job in the world.

After that Louis often went to Basin Street late at night to listen outside the cabaret where Ory's band was playing. Keeping an eye out for policemen, he lurked motionless in the shadows as long as he dared. During these hours he always experienced a mixture of enchantment and bitter frustration. All the way home he kept wishing himself back in the Colored Waifs' Home, playing in the band. What chance could he ever have to go on with music? He would never be able to save enough money to buy a cornet, and if he had one he would never have time to practice.

Late one evening, as he was walking slowly home from work, tired, dirty, and melancholy, a young man standing at the door of Matranga's saloon called to him as he went by. "Hey, Satchmo! Come on in!"

It was Clark Wade, the oldest boy in the quartet of minstrels that Louis had once led so gleefully. Wade knew all about Louis' success in the band at the Home and he knew the nickname that the boys had given him there. It made Louis feel happier just to hear that name again.

Wade was no longer one of Louis' close friends. He had acquired a reputation that was extremely bad, even for that section of New Orleans, now called the Battlefield. Louis, after his two discouraging years, could easily understand how it might be possible to sink into evil ways. Opportunities for good jobs simply did not exist for a Negro boy. Without ever consciously thinking about it, Louis knew that only his own good home and his loving relatives had saved him from the worst temptations.

Accepting Wade's invitation with a grin, Louis went into the saloon and joined him. For a long time the two sat talking about the old days. Louis realized how long he had been there when he saw the pianist and drummer who played for the evening customers enter the saloon. They were greeted by an anxious query from Matranga. "Where's Bunk?"

"Sick. He ain't showin' up tonight," was the laconic reply.

"What!" Matranga's voice rose in fury. "But I

got to have a trumpeter. What good are you two without one?" He banged his fist on the counter. "What am I going to do?" he shouted.

Clark Wade's voice sang out, "Well, look who's here, boss. You got a swell horn player right here. Satchmo played in the Waifs' Home band."

Louis smiled feebly. This was too sore a subject for joking. Matranga, however, walked over to the table and looked intently at the boy. "You was the leader in that Waifs' band, wasn't you?" he said. "Sure. I've heard you play in parades. What about this idea?"

Certain that both Clark and the saloonkeeper were merely amusing themselves, Louis said rather grumpily that he had played the cornet, not the trumpet, and anyway he had no cornet of his own.

"I'll go out and buy you one right now if you'll play it," urged Matranga quickly. "I got to have a horn blower. What about it?"

Startled by the sincerity of the offer, Louis stared at him. Yet he hesitated. Instinctively he pursed his lips as if around a mouthpiece. Those facial muscles were no longer firm. How could he play when he was so completely out of practice? Matranga was glaring at him. Sharply he shot out his ultimatum. "Make up your mind, kid. It's late."

Louis got to his feet, filled with apprehension. "All right," he muttered. "I'll try."

Matranga hurried to the door with Louis at his heels. In a nearby pawnshop they found a cornet, and after a long session of bargaining Matranga slapped down fifteen dollars and the instrument was placed in Louis' eager hands. He could hardly wait to blow it. But when he did so, back in the saloon, every fear was justified. His lips could not control the tone. Wavering, flatting, sliding, the uncertain notes of the cornet aroused groans, catcalls, and laughter from the patrons. Matranga scowled fiercely. It was no use. Louis laid down the cornet. In sudden desperation he stood up. They were playing the "Basin Street Blues." At least he could sing it.

Above the music of the piano and the beat of the drum rose the sound of Louis' sweet tenor voice. At the end of the song, everyone clapped, stamped, and yelled for more. The scowl faded from Matranga's face. Again and again Louis sang with the drum and piano. And when, in the early hours of the morning as he left for home, his employer gave him fifty cents and a sarcastic smile, Louis knew that only his songs had saved him from losing both his new cornet and his job.

"I got to do it!" he told himself. He recognized that this was his chance to enter the realm of jazz— through the back door, of course, but that made no difference. Every day that week he scrambled off the coal wagon at the noon hour, snatched up his cornet, and started practicing. Little by little the muscles of his lips grew stronger. Each night his playing sounded surer and more accurate.

Aware that he was trying his best, aware of the boy's talent, Matranga was patient. Before a month had passed, the cornetist he had hired in desperation was receiving applause from the patrons and often tips as well.

Now Louis was averaging little more than three hours of sleep each night, and it required all of Mamma Lucy's strength to shake him awake in the morning. He grew so desperately tired that he would fall asleep in the cart as he drove the patient mule. Only the excitement of playing the cornet kept him awake at Matranga's place in the evening.

One day it was his mother who roused him from sleep. He sat up and rubbed his eyes. Then he gave a shout of joy. "Mammy! I'm goin' right back to sleep. I don't have to git up. Dat ol' mule and de coal cart and me is parted for good and all."

"What?" His mother's voice showed her consternation. "How you goin' to git along den?"

"Look!" Louis fished from under his pillow a crumpled dollar bill and a fifty-cent piece. "I'll git this much every night. Soon I'll git more. Oh, Mammy, I'm goin' to earn my livin' wid dat cornet. Hallelujah in de mornin'!"

His mother's skeptical expression did not shake Louis' decision. He was having no more trouble with aching lips. His tone was clear and steady now. What he needed was time to practice. Already it was quite evident that he had become a definite asset at Matranga's place. The patrons found his radiant joy in the work contagious, and Matranga was pleased with the improvement in his playing.

Although Joe Oliver did not know it, Louis was receiving free instruction from him. Whenever Kid Ory's band played at the park, Louis went to listen and learn. His keen interest in Oliver's expert playing was untouched by envy now, for at last he himself was a part of the jazz world. He felt that his satisfaction would have been complete if only he could meet the great trumpeter.

At Matranga's saloon Louis was growing up fast. Although he had a boy's familiarity with the Battlefield characters, he never before had witnessed their behavior at close range. Often the scene was delightful. Merriment erupted in jokes, laughter, and marvels of inspired dancing. But gaiety could change in an instant into a dangerous drunken brawl.

One night a big, handsome woman called Mary Jack the Bear was holding court at the bar. Her majestic air and her readiness to fight off all rivals had prompted her admirers to call her Queen of the Battlefield. While the band played for the lively dancing in the center of the floor, Louis kept watching this extraordinary figure. All at once the saxophone player next him skipped a note to say loudly, "Look out!" Glancing toward the door, Louis caught sight of a young woman named Alberta slipping into the room and moving up to the bar.

At once Mary Jack the Bear turned to meet her.

Louis knew by their gestures and glaring eyes that the two women were exchanging deadly insults. It was not long before they were screaming at each other. Matranga, determined to prevent actual bloodshed if he could, rushed toward them. "Stop! Get out of here!" he yelled. The dancers stood still and the band was hushed. Matranga waved a hand at the musicians, shouting, "Go on, boys, play up!"

Louis hardly knew what he was playing. He was too intent on watching the two women, beside themselves with fury now, and Matranga's maneuvers as he headed them toward the door. Yelling and waving his arms, he drove them before him, and at last they were on the street.

Banging the door on their heels, the saloonkeeper leaned against it, panting. "Thank goodness I got them out!" he gasped. "Boys, you were great!" he said to the musicians. "You kept right on playing and that was a big help."

Louis was shaken by the violence of the scene and for a moment he wished he had another job. Naturally, that mood did not last. From every nook and corner of the Battlefield came evidence now that little Louis Armstrong had become the favorite horn player, and people came from other sections of New Orleans to hear him play and sing the blues. Of course Louis did not deceive himself. He was

only on the bottom rung of the ladder to success, but with ever-increasing confidence he played variations and solo parts which he had carefully practiced. Often he received in one evening a pocketful of bills given him as tips.

One night a wonderful event occurred. Joe Oliver came into the saloon. After he had been greeted by everyone, after Matranga had offered him refreshments, Oliver strolled over to the musicians' corner. Louis could feel his heart thumping with excitement. "Well, Satchmo," said the visitor, "I hear you're really good. So I came to listen myself. Go ahead now, boy!"

Matranga nodded. Many voices called out encouragement. As the piano ripped out the opening bars of "Are You from Dixie?" Louis began to play. Louder and louder, higher and higher, sounded his notes. The excitement of his mood pulsed through his playing and he held the last high note longer than ever before. Through the storm of applause, Joe Oliver hurried over. "Boy," he said, "that sure is something! Where'd you get those lips?"

Now Louis had his opportunity to express his unbounded admiration for Joe Oliver. He told him how he had spent hours listening to him play in

Kid Ory's band at the park and at the Storyville cabaret and how much he had learned from his playing.

"What?" Oliver shook his head. "What do you mean—the cabaret? You kids ain't allowed to go to that pleasure place."

Louis chuckled. "I went all right. I pulled my cap over my eyes and found a dark place outside where I could hear. And, man, can you blow!"

At this point yells arose from the patrons. "Joe Oliver!" "We want King Oliver!" "Joe, blow us a tune!" With a gracious wave of the hand Oliver strode to the piano, took up his trumpet, and, after a murmured word to pianist and drummer, sailed into "Panama." Louis crept close to listen and to watch the skillful fingering, the rise and fall of the big chest. At the end Louis joined in by singing the chorus. It was a glorious hour. Oliver's interest in Louis, winding up in a cordial invitation to come and see him the next day, lifted the boy's reputation several notches.

The meeting at Oliver's place was the beginning of a firm friendship between the two performers. Joe's wife made it plain that she had taken an instant liking to the boy. From then on he was often invited to meals at the Oliver home, where he heard long discussions of the ever-fascinating subject of jazz. In return he ran errands for Mrs. Oliver. When Kid Ory's band was hired for parades, Louis marched with them and carried Joe's trumpet between numbers. He soon became a favorite with every member of the band.

One afternoon when they were playing at the National Park, the drummer called out to the leader, "Hi, Ory, why don't you give the kid a chance to play?"

At Ory's smiling nod, the drummer sprang down and pushed the boy up on the platform. Thrilled but confident, Louis borrowed a cornet from one of the players and was ready when the signal was given him to join in playing a current blues piece. He saw out of the corner of his eye that Ory was giving him close attention. Without daring to glance at Joe Oliver, he felt that his friend was pouring out encouragement with every breath. When the last phrase faded away, Louis was trembling. He looked up to see the band leader standing over him. "Know what I think, little Louis?" said Ory. "I truly believe you're goin' to be a great horn player."

Perhaps as a result of this success, Joe Oliver suggested some weeks later that Louis substitute for him in the band while he was away for three days in Mobile. "Go see the cabaret proprietor," he said, "and tell him I sent you."

When Louis, dressed in the clothes he wore at Matranga's place, reported to the cabaret owner, the man looked him up and down with scornful amusement. "You might play right good if Joe thinks so, but you'd better come in a tuxedo tonight if you want the job."

Louis raced to a men's clothing store and was soon fitted out correctly. In the early evening Mamma Lucy danced around him in ecstasy. "Oh, Louis!" she cried. "You look mighty handsome in dem clo'es."

Louis took his place on the platform in the cabaret in Storyville that night and gazed around the big, gaudy room with dazzled eyes. He could hardly believe that he, the boy who had been chased out of Storyville so often by the police, was actually welcome there. In three days he was back at Matranga's saloon, possessed of a single ambition—to play in the District.

That was early in the summer of 1917. People in the Third Ward of New Orleans still talked of the wonderful Mardi Gras in March. Frolics, fights, affairs of the heart, went on as usual. But on Perdido Street there seemed to be little interest in what was happening on the world stage.

The United States, having declared war on Germany in April, had officially entered the terrible conflict. The entire nation was preparing for action. Young men were drilling in camps from the Atlantic to the Pacific Ocean. Factories on twenty-four-hour shifts were turning out munitions. Newspapers spread tales of battle and destruction across the country.

And then in September the World War came home to Louis Armstrong. First of all, there spread a rumor that city officials were going to close all the cabarets, saloons, and honky-tonks in the District and the Battlefield. For a time nobody believed it. But it was not long before saloon fronts were boarded up and the once lively streets were swept bare of pleasure seekers. Shortly thereafter Louis was called to the draft board, examined, listed, and given his number.

"Stop cryin', Mammy," he said almost angrily to his mother. "At least de gov'ment gives a man a job and money and sump'n' to eat. No place left anyway for a musician in dis here town. Dey're blackin' shoes and diggin' ditches an' cleanin' cars. You seen me put my tuxedo in de bottom of de chest and hang up my horn over my bed. Dat's where dey're goin' to stay till de Lawd knows when. I got a job down at de docks unloadin' cargo. I'd a heap rather be in de war. Maybe den I could join some army band. Anyways I figure I might learn sump'n'."

For a year and a day, however, Louis waited for that summons. Meanwhile, he drifted from job to job. Almost all of them required heavy physical labor that was too much for him. Finally he went back to selling coal from the wagon. He had no money to spend, no pleasures to enjoy except swimming in the river and very occasionally dropping in to see Joe Oliver. Joe was one of the few musicians in New Orleans who still had a job. Kid Ory's band was playing in the French Quarter. Louis, conscious of his calloused hands and his physical exhaustion, was so disheartened that he felt it was an imposition to thrust himself on Joe except very rarely.

Returning from his morning coal route one noon in November, Louis heard far down toward Canal Street the sound of the cathedral bell. Whistles began to blow. He saw that in the street a crowd was gathering and even from a distance the crowd looked strange. Were they dancing? Automobile horns started a continuous din. What on earth? Had the town gone crazy? Louis began to run. Catching sight of a lone man on Perdido Street, he asked him what was going on.

"It's peace," answered the old man. "De war's over, boy! Hallelujah!"

Hardly had Louis reached Canal Street when a snowstorm of torn paper floated down on him from an office window. Voices were screaming with laughter and shouts of joy. People were hugging each other and whirling about in mad circles. An acquaintance passing Louis yelled, "Git yo' horn, Satchmo! De war's over! Come sing an' play!"

Panting with excitement, Louis ran all the way home and snatched up his horn. For hours he sat practicing. What delight to be blowing again! And his lips had not lost their grip, as he had feared. At twilight he went racing about, trying to find a drummer and fiddler to join him in playing for the crowd. The streets were wild with gaiety. Lights streamed from doorways. Parades and dances replaced cars and trucks on the thoroughfares. Everyone's heart, like Louis' own, was bursting with joy and exhilaration. Rejoicing spread over the whole Western world that night.

Within a week the Battlefield had begun to regain its old life. Jazz was in demand again. Louis was busy almost every night at some club or dance hall. Glorying in his return to the world of music, he practiced harder than ever and his popularity soared. Now he felt free to pick up the threads of his friendship with the Olivers. Moreover, he was earning enough to round off a tempestuous love affair by marriage. Daisy Parker was the girl's name. She was pretty, audacious, and good fun.

Before the year ended Louis had a personal blow. He met Joe Oliver on the street one day in a state of great excitement. Snatching Louis' arm, Joe cried, "Satchmo, what you think? I got a bid to play in a hot-shot night club in Chicago. Big-town stuff, fella! Ain't that sump'n'?"

Louis tried to smile with pride at his friend's good luck, but his voice sounded like a wail as he said, "Oh, Papa Joe, are you goin' off to Chicago?"

That was indeed what happened. The Olivers were soon off and away. For some time Louis was disconsolate. Nowadays he did not look to Daisy for cheer and consolation, because the young couple had begun to quarrel. Daisy was jealous of Louis' music and lamented that she was wasting her youth on a husband who was out playing the cornet most of the night and asleep all of the morning. But she was her old radiant self when she heard the wonderful news Louis brought her one afternoon.

Pounding up the stairs and bursting into the room, Louis grinned so widely he could scarcely frame his words. "Daisy!" he shouted. "I'm second cornet in Kid Ory's band!" He grabbed his little wife around the waist and whirled her about the cluttered room in triumph.

This pleasant moment was almost the last one the two shared. Louis was soaring upward in his musical career. He was hired constantly now for parties in the French Quarter, for university dances, and for special occasions in cabarets and country clubs. All these engagements created further disagreement between him and his wife, and finally he left her and moved back to his mother's home.

Mardi Gras that year was a great occasion for Louis. His growing fame was demonstrated when he was chosen as a courtier to the king of the Zulus. The Zulus were a Negro organization that parodied and poked fun at the elaborate Mardi Gras celebrations of the white people of New Orleans. The beautiful yacht on which the white king of the Mardi Gras was borne to the foot of Canal Street was matched by an ancient barge carrying the Zulu monarch. The white Mardi Gras king sat in glory on a throne built upon a magnificently decorated float pulled through the streets by white horses. He was gaily mocked by the flimsy mule-drawn chariot that bore the ruler of the Zulus.

Dressed in tinseled robes as one of the king's attendants, Louis laughed and clowned and acted his comedy part to the hilt. It had been an honor to be admitted to the Zulu organization, but the best part was all the hilarity and the fun. Louis enjoyed every minute of it.

In the 1920's, when Louis Armstrong was winning a distinguished place in the world of jazz, many other Negro musicians—Roland Hayes and Marian Anderson, for example—had already risen to great prominence. Their interest was chiefly in classical music, but they also delighted their audiences by singing the beautiful old Negro spirituals. H. T. Burleigh had achieved fame by his skillful arrangements of these songs and by his interpretations of them. Singers from Fisk University had been traveling throughout the United States and in Europe for years. But these artists were completely apart from the vigorous upsurge of jazz. As for the creators of the new musical idiom, struggling upward as they were from the depths of poverty, they had no chance at all to hear these highly trained artists of their own race. Indeed, they hardly knew about them.

Not long after the Mardi Gras, however, Louis Armstrong had his first glimpse of one young colored woman who was just rising to fame as an actress. A show came to New Orleans with Ethel Waters as star performer. Louis not only saw the show, which he applauded till his hands were sore, he met the star and found her a simple, friendly person, who seemed delighted by his enthusiasm. She introduced him to Fletcher Henderson, her accompanist, who was also helping to direct the show. This young man was so convinced of the importance of jazz in the realm of music that he had given up a teaching career to devote himself to its promotion.

As long as the show remained in New Orleans, Henderson went about to listen to the jazz bands. Time and time again he turned up at the cabaret where Louis was playing, and between numbers they talked together about the new music.

"You play the cornet the way I like it played, Armstrong," said the pianist. "You have the true jazz swing and a real genius for variation. Your high notes are marvelous!"

Charmed by praise from such a source, Louis said, "Well, as I see it, a jazz player should be turned loose to improvise. He's got to play de way he feels."

Louis had fun for a time organizing his own little band to play for clubs and dances. He enjoyed a bit of clowning between numbers, and the adventure helped him forget his troubles with Daisy. She was both bitter and resentful, and whenever he saw her he felt ashamed of the sordid outcome of his impulsive marriage. For this reason he was emotionally ready for a change of environment. Yet when his first opportunity came, he hesitated.

A letter arrived from Fletcher Henderson. He had recently organized a jazz band that was playing in New York City, and he invited Louis to join it as cornetist. As he read, Louis felt cold chills down his spine in spite of his excitement. New York! The very sound of it was terrifying. To be off there, far from his family and friends and everything he had ever known! Oh, no! Then he hit upon a possibility that would make the move less difficult. He wrote Henderson that if he could take a friend of his along who played the drum he would brave New York. After an uneasy wait, Henderson's reply settled the question. He did not feel that he could fire his own good drummer to accommodate Louis. With friendly mutual regrets the matter ended.

But Louis' restlessness persisted. Only now and then did he feel carefree and full of zest. That was, however, just his mood one evening when Kid Ory's band set off in a truck to advertise a big public dance. Driving slowly through the streets with their advertising banners, the band played a series of popular tunes with all their might. Passers-by applauded, cheered, and exchanged jokes with the players.

All at once, as the truck turned into one of the narrowest streets, another truck, with a band advertising a different entertainment, came chugging up from the opposite direction. Neither party would yield the right of way. There followed a musical duel loud enough to arouse the Voodoo Queen

Marie herself from her stone tomb miles away. Louis stood up and blew his high, piercing notes until he felt as though his lungs would burst. Largely due to his powerful volume of sound, the second truck finally admitted defeat and backed away.

Just as Louis fell back on his seat in exhausted triumph, he heard his name called from the sidewalk. A young man stepped from the curb to the side of the truck. "Hi, Louis!" he shouted. "Come down here a moment. I want to talk to you."

"Why hello, Fate Marable!" Louis exclaimed. "Where'd you drop from?" As he clambered down from the truck, he wondered what the pianist wanted of him.

Fate Marable had been conducting a band on an excursion boat that made trips up and down the Mississippi River. This year, it seemed, he was reorganizing his band. "I'm collecting a twelve-piece band, Satchmo," he said quickly, "and I need a cornetist. I've never heard anybody play the cornet the way you do, and I want you to sign up with me."

There it was, thought Louis, with racing pulse. Just what he had wanted for years. He knew the excursion boats made only evening trips all winter and tied up at Canal Street every midnight. Here was no frightening, lonely venture to a strange city. Of course, he would hate to leave Kid Ory's outfit, which had taught him so much. But as part of a really important band conducted by an experienced musician, he could learn still more. Then and there he accepted the proposal.

It was a bright November day when Louis first climbed aboard the *Dixie Belle*. She was a handsome stern-wheeler with wide, open decks and a dance floor occupying the center of the ship. Louis received a warm welcome from the other members of the band. Most of them were top New Orleans in-

strumentalists, whom he knew well. All agreed that it was fine to work with a gifted musician like Marable. Besides being master of the piano, he had that knowledge of all the other instruments and of the score essential to a good conductor.

Louis was happy that winter. He had time to see his friends and family. Sometimes he even took Daisy out for a good time and she did her best to make him forget their unhappy quarrels.

To float along the river, playing for a gay crowd of dancers who loved jazz, seemed to him an entrancing way of making a living. Louis only needed to hear a piece once to be able to play it, embroider on it, and work it up to a climax in his own individual style. The programs were interesting, for Marable was always introducing new compositions. Of course, W. C. Handy's "St. Louis Blues" was a great favorite. Its insertion of a tango beat within the African rhythm was a fascinating innovation.

In April Marable told his men that the summer schedule would begin in a week. This meant that the *Dixie Belle* would make her slow way north to the very source of the Mississippi. Already it was too hot on the glassy river to attract large crowds for the evening excursions. "We sail next Monday morning," said the conductor. "Everybody be ready on time."

Louis heard this with joy. He well remembered once telling Peter Davis at the Waifs' Home that his idea of bliss was to take a trip to the river's source as cornetist in a ship's band. Miraculously, the wish was coming true. On shore he was showered with congratulations. "You'll see Memphis and St. Louis!" said his friends. "Show 'em, Satchmo, how New Orleans jazz cats play!"

A crowd came to see the ship sail. Louis' mother and Mamma Lucy were on the Canal Street dock, blowing kisses and waving handkerchiefs. Leaning over the rail, Louis Armstrong looked down at them with his widest smile. Now, for the first time, he was going to sample the great world outside New Orleans. With whistle blowing and paddle wheel frantically whirling, the *Dixie Belle* moved up the mighty stream.

4. "Deep River"

New Orleans had long disappeared from view before Louis could take a look at the river. He had been busy getting settled in his quarters and chatting with his fellow musicians. When he broke away and stepped out alone on the forward deck, a wave of happiness swept over him.

It was a windless morning. Sunshine flooded the water and lazy clouds flung down white radiance upon the shining surface. Looking straight below, Louis could feel the power of the current pushing against the ship's bow. Here, as the Mississippi rushed toward the Gulf, it had narrowed and deepened. Above the high levees on either bank scattered houses could be seen, pale against brilliant green stretches of sugar cane, and an occasional lofty chimney marked a huge refining plant.

The river traffic was fascinating to watch. A large tugboat pushing several laden barges tooted cheerfully at a flotilla of fishing scows. Against the banks, half hidden by cypress and cottonwood saplings, shanty boats were tied up. One, decorated with a line of drying wash, added a splash of color to the scene. Close to the *Dixie Belle* a sleek yacht suddenly shot past, a streak of white on the dark water. Beneath all this vivid human activity Louis felt the will of the great river—ancient, mysterious, alien.

Gradually the steady throb of the ship's engines cast over Louis a delicious drowsiness. Unresisting, he curled up in the sun behind the pilothouse. Before closing his eyes, however, he drew from its case a brand-new cornet. He gazed upon it lovingly, polished it with a woolen cloth, and blew a few triumphant notes before tucking it away again. Then, cuddling his treasure beside him, he drifted off to sleep.

At Baton Rouge, eighty miles up the winding river, the tour was initiated. At dusk that evening Louis first experienced the routine of the *Dixie Belle's* well-staged arrival. The band, dressed in uniform, stood in formation on the main deck. While the town was still far away, a crowd could be seen massed on the brilliantly lighted wharf. Indeed, all Baton Rouge seemed to sparkle with lights.

A bell tinkled signals for landing. The big paddle wheels churned in foaming reverse. Then from the main cabin screamed a blast of high-pitched, strident melody.

With a violent start, Louis shouted to the man next him, "What's dat noise?"

His companion laughed. "The calliope!" he shouted back. "Marable's playin' it to tell the folks we've come. He loves it."

Half a minute after the last note of "The Bluebells of Scotland" had shrieked overhead, Fate Marable, smart in his white linen suit, appeared before the band. "Okay?" he demanded, and lifted his baton. Louis noticed how swiftly the conductor's eyes swept over each man to assure complete readiness. The introductory number had been decided at rehearsal.

Down came Marable's slender hands, and through the soft air floated the first bars of "Tiger Rag." Above the rim of his horn Louis caught a glimpse of hats and handkerchiefs waving, and even through the music he heard roars of joyous greeting.

There was no staying to watch the people embark. The musicians bolted to their messroom to fortify themselves for the work ahead. When they were summoned to the dance floor above, Louis looked appreciatively over the gay throng. It was identical with the dancing crowds he had watched all winter, but there was fresh zest in playing for these people. Baton Rouge was close enough to New Orleans to follow the progress of jazz in the Crescent City. The response of those firstcomers to the *Dixie Belle,* as the elaborated melodies wove around the steady drumbeat, was intoxicating to the players. Louis heard it summed up by one pretty girl's exclamation: "I could just die dancin' to those blues!"

Midnight ended the entertainment. As the crowd made its way down the gangplank, Louis said to the drummer, "Let's get some cold ginger ale an' set on deck awhile."

"Not me!" was the reply. "I'm heavin' into my bunk. I'm tired. Ain't you?"

After a band performance Louis always felt excited and keyed up, ready for diversion rather than sleep. To his surprise, he was absolutely alone in this feeling. Not a man would linger on deck with him. On his reluctant way to the band's sleeping quarters he met Fate Marable and stopped hopefully.

"Turning in, Satchmo?" said Marable. "Good idea! Tomorrow we rehearse and play for afternoon and evening excursions. We all need sleep."

As Louis slipped off his clothes he thought longingly of the nights last winter after the evening excursions, when he had always hurried from the ship to some cabaret. Listening to the band, dancing and

gossiping with friends, had often been followed by
one of those glorious sessions with half a dozen fellow musicians working up new jazz themes. How
could he bear a nightly program of sleep at the ab-
surd hour of twelve? He stayed awake just long
enough to ask himself the question.

It was answered the next morning. Breakfast was
served at eight, and whoever failed to be present had
nothing to eat until lunch. The morning rehearsal
and both afternoon and evening excursions required
hours of playing. On his second night aboard Louis
was one of the first in bed.

As the *Dixie Belle* set off for Natchez, something
happened that was to have great importance in
Louis Armstrong's musical career. After rehearsal,

he was putting away his cornet when a soft voice said, "Wait a minute, Satchmo!"

Beside him stood one of the members of the band, a tall, rangy man named David Jones. He played the mellophone, a curious big horn with many coils. His pleasant manners had attracted Louis from the first and his intelligent musicianship was admired by everyone. It was quite an honor to be singled out for talk by this quiet individual.

"Satchmo," Jones began, "I surely admire your playing. I know one reason it's so good is because you never let those lip and jaw muscles sag. That's great. But, Satchmo," he went on, "I notice sump'n' funny. I got to ask you—'cause I think I could help you. Satchmo, can you read music?"

Louis was startled by the question. He dropped his head and muttered, "Well, not so good."

"Maybe you mean just plain no. I watched you through two rehearsals when Fate passed out new arrangements. You couldn't make nothin' of the sheet music and had to wait till the rest of us played it through. Boy, what an ear you got! One in a million! But that ain't enough. If you want to go places in band work, you just got to learn to read."

"I know it," Louis replied gravely. "I jes' ain't had no chance to study."

"Lots of slick jazz players do it all by ear," Jones

said sympathetically. "But, Satchmo, you got talent. You can't stop there. I could teach you to read if you'd let me."

"Let you!" Louis waved his cornet case in the air. "Would you really do dat, Davy? Leave us start right now!"

Then and there began Louis' introduction to the mysteries of those flag-bearing black dots called notes. His eagerness to learn made him a rewarding pupil, and the two friends made a pact to work every single day.

Tired but exhilarated by the first lesson, Louis stepped out on deck. He found that the ship was pursuing a zigzag course which took her almost from bank to bank. Here the Mississippi swept in enormous curves, so sharp that sometimes one could hardly see the river half a mile ahead. Long sand bars rose glistening from the cocoa-colored water. Absorbed in the scene, Louis was startled to find the ship's captain standing beside him.

"You seem to watch our course right closely, young fellow," drawled the captain.

Until this moment the wiry old man with the white beard and bushy eyebrows had seemed remote and unfriendly. But now he was smiling affably.

"Yes, sir." Louis flashed his brilliant smile. "I'm

tryin' to figure out why you cross de river so much
and how you dast turn up little side creeks so close
to dem islands."

A deep chuckle answered him. "The Mississippi
is a shifty character, my boy. The pilot's got to learn
all her tricks. If one of those cutoffs is deep enough,
we may save a lot of miles by slipping through it.
As for our course, the worst reefs are often right in
midstream and we have to swing with the channel.
The pilot's got a hard job—even now with all the
engineering that's been done. Nobody ever described it better than a pilot named Samuel Clem-

ens. He took to writing under another name. Ever read *Life on the Mississippi* by Mark Twain?"

"Mark Twain? Why, he's de man wrote *Huckleberry Finn*. My teacher gave it to me. Did you ever see dat pilot, Captain?"

The question drew an elated answer. When the captain was a very little boy, his father had taken him aboard Mr. Clemens' ship, which was tied up at the town where he lived. They found the pilot sitting in a canvas chair smoking a long, black cigar.

"He took me right on his knee," boasted the captain, "and then into the pilothouse to see the compass. He even let me shift the steering wheel. I'll never forget him. He had a big mustache and a twinkle in his eye. A young fellow, he was then. That was the man who became famous all over the world for his books!"

After the *Dixie Belle* had tied up at Natchez, there was time before dark for Louis to climb the high bluffs and take a look at the city. He could see the spire of St. Mary's Cathedral and the bulky shape of college buildings. He strolled past the beautiful old houses, many of them shabby and forlorn now. Giant wisteria and climbing roses had turned iron fences into walls of luxuriant color.

On his return to the wharves he paused to watch the roustabouts loading cotton bales on a big barge.

Remembering his own backbreaking hours at this job, he marveled to hear the men joking, laughing, and singing as if they were playing a game. A surge of gratitude for his own good luck swept over him.

A large crowd came aboard for the evening sail and dance. After the third number, one of the ship's mates strolled up to the orchestra platform. "Can your boys play a wedding march, Marable?" he asked.

"Why, yes, I guess so," the band leader answered.

"Well," the mate went on, "there's a couple here had the notion to get married on board. Brought a minister and all. Bad luck to have a minister on board, but he's here. So when I give the signal, start up."

The ship's officers organized the ceremony with efficiency. Presently the pretty young bride came in on her father's arm between rows of people massed on either side. Groom and best man waited beside the minister. The affair went off with surprising dignity.

After the final wedding march, the band swung into jazz and everyone on the floor swirled into a lively dance. Louis, blowing piercing soprano variations of the melodies, thought he had never seen so gay a party.

But what was happening? He saw people suddenly crowding to the door. Faces looked aghast. Shrieks stopped the music. Then he heard repeated on deck the cry that had shattered the gaiety—"Man overboard!" He felt the *Dixie Belle* reduce her speed to a crawl and then go into reverse.

Fate Marable's imperious gesture checked the musicians as they started to follow the rush of the crowd to the rail. A medley of cries and shouts tore the night. All at once Louis felt himself sliding. The ship was listing. In a flash he thought, Two hundred people on one side of the boat! It's going over! He heard the mates bawling, "Back! Get back from the rail!" An officer stuck his head in the window and yelled, "Marable, play something! Quick!"

"Play 'Dixie'!" cried Marable and flung himself down at the piano.

Shaken though they were, the men blared out the tune. Slowly men and women drifted back to the dance floor. Slowly the ship righted herself. In a far corner the wedding party gathered around the little bride. When the band stopped playing, Louis heard her sobbing. Only then did the whispered meaning of the tragic episode reach his ears. The man who had jumped overboard into the swift current was the bride's heartbroken discarded suitor.

A pale, disheveled mate gave brief details. "Only one deckhand saw him jump. We tried throwing life preservers, but he just disappeared. The current took him right off. That minister! Every river man knows it's bad luck havin' one aboard. And those dumb idiots! I fair had to club 'em back from the rail. Thought sure we was goin' over." Shaking his head, he stumbled away.

There was no combating the melancholy pervading the ship. Louis leaned over Marable, slumped down on the piano bench. "Dancing's out, Fate. Why don't we play some stuff like 'Swanee River' or 'There's a Long, Long Trail'?"

Marable nodded, and the *Dixie Belle* made her subdued way back to Natchez, with the band playing mournful strains.

After breakfast the next morning, Louis observed that the ship was still steaming through the bayou country. To the west, little lakes where wild ducks floated were always in view. Great white cranes flew from one stretch of land to another and fishing craft dotted the countryside. Seems like Louisiana must be half under water, he thought.

Propping himself in his favorite place back of the pilothouse, he laboriously scribbled a picture post card of Natchez for Mamma Lucy. She would laugh, he knew, if he could tell her all he was learning on the trip—other things as well as reading music. Somebody was forever pumping him full of history about how the French once owned Louisiana and how their missionaries were the first to paddle down the Mississippi. Proof of this was written on the maps in the French names of towns and creeks. A deck hand told him that fishermen on the islands in the bayous spoke mostly French even then.

At Vicksburg it was Civil War tales that Louis heard. In July of 1863, Ulysses S. Grant had forced the surrender of the fort on the bluffs at Vicksburg and won absolute control of the Mississippi. To conquer the brave defenders, the Union general had to lay siege to the place. The starving villagers survived terrible bombardments from Union gunboats by living in caves dug out of the steep cliffs.

Since the *Dixie Belle* lingered for two days at Vicksburg, Louis and David Jones had time to explore the old city. Its bustling prosperity as shipping center of the region offered no hint of a tragic past. Once it had stood directly on the river. But the wayward Mississippi had moved so far away that a deep canal had to be dug to connect town and river, and now railroads hauled more of the cotton crop than the river barges did.

After a stop at Greenville, Mississippi, and at Phillips on the other side of the river in Arkansas, Louis tingled with the anticipation of seeing Memphis, the Tennessee city that claimed to be the birthplace of the blues.

Memphis gave the *Dixie Belle* a welcome of stunning proportions. Every afternoon and evening throngs of people came to dance and enjoy the band. One night the members of a lodge chartered the boat and defied all custom by bringing its own band to play. Dumbfounded, the ship's musicians saw the white players stride up to the dance platform with their horns and drums.

Uneasily Louis watched Marable, tense with fury, cross the floor to the lodge band leader. He was afraid the high-strung intensity that made Marable a superior pianist and conductor might catapult him into a dangerous row. But Fate proved to have a gentleman's self-control. With icy courtesy he waved the intruders to their place.

"Our services are not wanted tonight, boys," he called to his own band. "Take those seats against the wall."

It was comforting to find that the lodge band was utterly commonplace. Indeed, members of the *Dixie Belle* were even somewhat disappointed in the colored jazz bands they heard when they visited the honky-tonks on Beale Street. Although the boast of Memphis was that the blues had been born there—thanks to the nationally popular compositions of W. C. Handy, the "St. Louis Blues" and the "Beale Street Blues"—jazz had not developed in that city as it had in New Orleans. Marable said the explanation lay in the fact that colored bands were not hired to play in the clubs and hotels of Memphis.

Louis spent the next days of the northern journey in working harder than ever on his music lessons. Jones was not only teaching him to read, he was also teaching him to phrase with truer tone values. The pupil had begun to realize how far he still had to go before reaching excellence.

After only one more stop the ship reached Cairo. Situated at the southern tip of Illinois, at the junction of the Ohio and Mississippi Rivers, it is the meeting place of two other states, Missouri and Ken-

tucky. Turbulent waters foam around two sides of
the city and in flood time are likely to inundate
parts of it. Southward to the Gulf the powerful
stream is called the Lower Mississippi. North of
Cairo the states bordering on the river lose their
Southern character, for the old Southern traditions
were engulfed long ago by the pioneering life of
the West.

What Louis Armstrong enjoyed most about the
stop at Cairo were the excursions up the Ohio River.
The party went as far as Paducah, Kentucky. The
sight of rolling, lush green fields made it plain why
pioneers had been lured into Kentucky two cen-
turies before. It was hot on the river by that time.
Playing hour after hour left the musicians drenched
and weary. Yet never were their spirits gayer, for at
last they were approaching St. Louis. Every one of
them knew that never before had an all-Negro band
visited the city. Each man was primed to outdo his
best.

The landing at dusk was impressive. Every single
light on the *Dixie Belle* was blazing. From the forward deck the band sent over the levee wave after
wave of sound as they played the "St. Louis Blues."
Yet, blow as they might, they could not drown the
roar of welcome from the vast waiting crowd.

Passengers on those first expeditions had spread

the fame of Fate Marable's band. Soon individual musicians were invited to play solos as guest performers with the best bands in the city. Louis Armstrong was in transports of joy to be chosen, with Fate and Davy Jones, as a guest artist at the most fashionable cabaret. As they taxied through brightly lighted streets, past handsome shop windows and towering hotels, Louis was speechless with excitement.

The band leader at the cabaret received them with the reverential cordiality fitting for princes of the jazz realm. "I've done my best, Mr. Marable," he said, "to keep up with progress in jazz, but I know we can't match you fellows from New Orleans."

Sipping their iced drinks, the visiting trio gazed judiciously about the crowded room. To men who had played at the country clubs and restaurants of New Orleans, the patrons seemed to lack a certain elegance. As for the visitors' opinion of the band, their reactions were summed up by David Jones. Thoughtfully stroking his chin, he remarked, "My heart sure aches for them poor white boys. It's like they was used to old nags and were suddenly tryin' to cope with mustangs."

After about an hour, the band leader invited his guests to play. Marable warned him that although only three members of his band could hardly do it justice, they would do their best. Smiling and curious, the men in the cabaret band moved back. The conductor shouted, "Ladies and gentlemen!" In the silence that followed he introduced the three "distinguished performers from the famous Crescent City," and named each one. Polite applause preceded an absorbed hush.

Marable began the strong beat of a new hot song. Davy and Louis blew with every trick of phrasing, pause, and melodic variation known to experts. Louis' high notes rose to an almost incredible pitch. Bedlam broke out when they finished. Cheers, clapping, and stamping wound up in cries of "More! More!"

Next they played the "St. Louis Blues." Slim young Louis, lips parted in a merry smile, white teeth gleaming against his dark skin, was obviously the favorite. His name was shouted again and again. Bowing shyly, he felt dizzy with this public triumph in a northern city.

Later, the guests were ushered into the conductor's dressing room to discuss jazz compositions and new techniques. The host inquired about Kid Ory of New Orleans and reported that King Oliver was "making a mighty big hit in Chicago"—a comment that delighted Louis.

Although it was almost morning when Louis finally tumbled into bed, he lay sleeplessly reviewing the evening's sensational success. To have shared such an experience with Fate and Davy was a privilege he would never forget. Wonderingly he recalled a forlorn boy perched on a mule cart, calling out, "Coal here, ladies! Five cents a bucket!" Had he really been that boy only two years ago?

Never during the *Dixie Belle's* stay at St. Louis did the band's popularity flag. In twos and threes, its members played after midnight at hotels, clubs, and cabarets. The Fourth of July, however, was set aside for a special party to celebrate Louis Armstrong's twentieth birthday. Satchmo was offered enthusiastic toasts as the coming horn blower of the world.

By the time the ship started north again, everyone was exhausted by late hours and excitement. Rejoicing greeted the news that only one stop was scheduled on the five-hundred-mile run to St. Paul. After spending several days and nights catching up on sleep, Louis returned eagerly to his music lessons. Except for them, he felt lonely and bored for the first time on this trip.

It was excruciatingly hot. The glare from the river hurt the eyes. One afternoon the drummer organized a desperate plan for relief. A long rope fastened under a man's arms and tied firmly to a deck stanchion would permit a cooling dip without risk. Hardly had the ropes been secured when eight swimmers were kicking and splashing in the river. As he cavorted in the current, Louis shouted a chant he had picked up from the roustabouts.

"River was so deep and wide
    I couldn't call my baby from de other side."

Suddenly a sharp whistle blew from the lower deck. One of the mates leaned over the taffrail to roar through a megaphone, "Up on deck! Every man of you on the double-quick!"

There was no disputing that command. Faster than they would have believed possible, the swimmers dragged themselves hand over hand up the ropes and stood dripping on deck.

"You blamed fools!" roared the mate. "Ain't you never seen what drifts in the river? Suppose a big snag flies up at you! Or a plank, likely with nails in it! Your guts would be ripped outa you. You oughta have more sense!"

To offset the sheepishness of his companions, Louis thanked the mate politely and added, "Anyways, we was also in danger of cookin' in dat water. Ain't nothin' cool 'bout dat Mississippi."

A few nights later, at about eleven o'clock, the

same mate strode into the messroom, where Louis was playing poker with a few others. "Armstrong!" he sang out. "Captain wants to see you in the pilot-house."

With a startled look Louis slapped down his cards and followed the mate along the deck. "What's he want of me?" he asked anxiously.

"Dunno." The tone suggested the direst possibilities. Pointing up the ladder to the pilothouse, the mate murmured, "Just hope for the best!"

As Louis stepped into the dark interior of the pilothouse, the captain turned from his post behind the man at the wheel. Beckoning to Louis, he said, "Look ahead now! We're just coming to Jackson's Island."

For an instant Louis was baffled. Then he remembered their conversation about Mark Twain. Jackson's Island was the place where Huckleberry Finn hid away after his supposed murder and where he found Jim, the runaway slave. So that was all the captain wanted! Intently, as if a heartfelt wish were being granted, Louis stared into the misty distance. The river spread out like a huge lake. Only vague shadows marked its boundaries.

"Where is dat island, Captain?"

"Straight ahead, boy. Use your eyes."

Sure enough—a dark mass of land suddenly appeared in the ship's brilliant searchlight. Now they were skirting the island so closely that drooping willow branches smacked the ship and its passage sent waves thundering over the banks and beaches.

"Great place for those fellows to hide, wasn't it?" chuckled the captain. "I knew you'd like to see it."

"Yes, sir! Much obliged, Captain. How can you pick anything out o' dis darkness in time to miss it?"

"Oh, we know every island in the river. We know when the Mississippi takes a notion to move one of 'em or swallow one up." The captain touched Louis' arm. "Look at those little lights way across there. That's Hannibal, Missouri, where Mark Twain grew up. By daylight you can see the high bluffs. Guess that town's pretty proud to claim such a writer."

Next day they were to make a stop at Quincy, Illinois. Louis and several others spent hours watching the river. The water was low and the ship was cautiously poking her way between long sand bars.

One of the deck hands said, "In my twenty years on this river I never seen so many sand bars. It'll be a miracle if we don't git grounded."

Landing ceremonies at Quincy had to undergo a sudden change. The band was lining up as usual when everyone noticed that the crowd on the wharf had a band of its own. The faint sound of a Sousa march was wafted toward the ship.

"Ain't that nice and cordial of 'em to serenade us!" cried Davy Jones. "I reckon they heard from St. Louis what jazz cats we are."

The moonlight sail from Quincy was long remembered. During the band's ten o'clock intermission Louis stepped out on deck to enjoy the faint breeze. Pointing out a mass of dark clouds, he asked a deck hand if they meant rain and was told that they certainly did.

The music for the next dance had hardly begun when a cloudburst hit the ship. Lightning tore the clouds. Thunder crashed and rumbled. As the guests rushed into the dance hall, wind roared in with them. Campstools slithered noisily around the deck. Men struggled to close cabin windows. The ship pitched and rolled so violently that people slid off their seats. Louis' mind flew to the pilothouse, where the old captain must be trying to hold the ship in the channel.

A sudden tremendous bump threw everyone to the floor. The *Dixie Belle* shook and trembled. Then she bucked forward and back like a bronco. Cries of fear came from the crowd. "We're on the bottom!" yelled a voice.

Springing to the platform, Fate Marable shouted, "Come on, men! Play 'Tiger Rag'!"

It did not matter that all the music racks were flat on the floor. Everyone knew the piece by heart and played it with desperate gaiety. The last measures were all but lost in a bellow from the mate's megaphone. "Don't be scared, folks! This ship's as sound as a bell. We're on a sand bar, but there's no danger. If anybody's nervous, grab a life preserver here by the door."

As the band began to play again, two girls ran to the door, snatched up life preservers, and, stepping into them, began a grotesque dance. Laughter rippled through the cabin. But with torrents of rain still falling and gales shaking the ship, few dared venture to their feet. Doggedly the musicians kept on with their work.

At midnight another mate appeared to announce regretfully that there could be no return to Quincy that night. The cook, he said, was preparing sandwiches and hot coffee in the galley. He thanked the guests for their good spirits and repeated that they had nothing to fear.

The musicians all volunteered to help pass the refreshments. Louis amused the young people by an exaggerated take-off of a haughty waiter. At last the storm passed on. Windows were flung open.

When the passengers had settled themselves as comfortably as possible, the lights were turned low. On their way to their quarters, the bandsmen learned that the rudder chains had broken in the storm and repairs must be made before the ship could be maneuvered off the bar.

With the sun bright and the water quiet the next morning, nobody could be afraid. But anxiety had shifted to the folks at home, who must be wild with worry. Louis helped serve the breakfast of corn bread, coffee, and rice. He pretended not to notice the odd appearance of people in rumpled evening clothes at that early morning hour.

It was night before the *Dixie Belle* finally landed her passengers. From a distance could be seen lanterns and flashlights along the riverbanks and far out on the water. "Searchers!" Fate Marable muttered to Louis. "The whole town thinks the ship was lost in the storm."

At sight of the ship's lights, a huge crowd came rushing to the wharf. Cheers, sobs, and wild embraces greeted the weary passengers at the gangplank.

That long delay at Quincy was fatal to Marable's hope of reaching St. Paul in time for the Labor Day vacation crowds. Steam as he would, the captain could not land there until too late for an evening sail. The ship stayed there a few days to make the scheduled excursions, but it was too cold at night now to attract large crowds.

No one was sorry when the *Dixie Belle* headed south on the three-thousand-mile voyage to New Orleans. Stops were few and short on the return trip. Only at St. Louis was the band's original experience recaptured with a similar thrill. But at last came the ecstatic moment when the distant outlines of New Orleans shimmered in the afternoon sun.

Louis leaned over the rail, tense with expectation. Yet now that the journey was over, he realized all it had meant—interesting contacts, expanded knowledge of his country, memorable scenes of beauty, and, above all else, his first basic steps toward mastery of the music that was now the core of his life.

5. *Climbing the Scale*

Louis' mother and Mamma Lucy were on the Canal Street dock to greet him, but Daisy was not. However, for several weeks after Louis' return to New Orleans, it seemed as if all his former differences with Daisy had dissolved. Louis sometimes took his pleasure-loving little wife to afternoon picnics. Often after a session on the *Dixie Belle* they went to cabarets together. But somehow Louis could no longer find the same gaiety in the old haunts. The only way he could really enjoy them was to take his cornet along and join the band now and then.

Daisy realized with resentment that her husband had grown beyond her. Jealous of the time he spent at solo practice and on the ship, she began to quarrel with him again in her violent way. Reconciliations did not last. Finally the two mistaken young people decided to part for good. Louis was glad when April came and with it another six months' tour up and down the Mississippi.

When the ship returned to New Orleans, Louis left the band. He was tired of traveling and believed that in order to advance as a jazz musician he needed a different connection. Although Fate Marable bemoaned the loss of his top cornet player, he generously agreed that the decision was wise.

The speed with which Louis found an engagement in town was proof of his growing reputation. Word spread about the jazz world of New Orleans that he was free, and in a few days a message reached him that Tom Anderson wanted to see him at his cabaret.

As Louis walked along on the afternoon of the appointment, his mind raced back to a similar errand four years before, in August, 1917. His great ambition that year was to play in the District, and Tom Anderson had half promised him a chance to try for his band. But when he went to sign up for the job, he had found the manager in the doldrums. Pressure from the wartime Federal government upon the government of Louisiana, and on down to the mayor and council of New Orleans, had resulted in an order that all saloons, cabarets, and honky-tonks must close. Louis had heard that day that there would be no job for him because there would be no cabaret. The young man of twenty-one could feel again the bitter dismay that had stabbed the seventeen-year-old boy. He wondered what he would think of that boy's playing if he could hear it now. Bet it was punk, he thought.

Anderson was waiting for him near the side door. "Well, Louis Armstrong!" he boomed. "Things sure are different for both of us since the last time you came here. Remember when you wanted a job in my band? Okay, it's ready for you now—four years later, but with almost four times the pay I would have offered you then. Come on in. I've redecorated my place. And believe me, Satchmo, I got a swell lot of patrons now."

When Louis returned that evening to play, he found the boast justified. Anderson had an attractive cabaret and a well-behaved clientele. Best of all, the band could play true jazz. The musicians were eager to support Armstrong's inspired improvisations and proud to feature his solo flights.

To have nothing to do all day but sleep, practice, go swimming at Lake Pontchartrain, and enjoy his family and friends, was delightful for a while. Nevertheless, when the energetic Louis was asked to join the Tuxedo Marching Band, he accepted instantly. It was fun to be in parades and to play at picnics. In short, it was always fun to play the cornet. Thus winter slipped gently into the magnolia and camellia season. Yet the young man sometimes wondered whether he was fated to remain forever attached to this familiar southern city where he had spent almost all his days.

As he marched with the band one blistering July afternoon, Louis' mind was occupied once more with thoughts of the future. The band had been acting as escort to members of an important lodge and was returning to its quarters. To the joy of the youngsters on Rampart Street, who were all shouting the chorus, it was playing "Oh, Didn't He Ramble!" Smiling faces appeared at windows. On the curb a bare-legged girl with bandanna-bound head saluted the marchers by pretending to offer them her tray of fresh peaches.

With a piercing final blast, the band reached the lodge hall. Louis, to his great surprise, saw Mamma Lucy pushing her way through the gathering crowd, waving a yellow envelope. "Telegram for you, Louis!" she cried.

"What?" he exclaimed. "I don't believe it!" But he reached for the envelope and tore it open.

His shout of surprise brought the band members clustering around him with excited questions. When they heard what the telegram said, cheers of congratulations burst forth. It was from Joe Oliver, asking Louis to come to Chicago at once to join his band at Lincoln Gardens.

"Hurrah for Satchmo!"

"King Oliver signed it hisse'f! It's true!"

Only the band leader was downcast. "When you going, Satchmo?" he asked mournfully.

"Jes' as soon as I can git a train to Chicago," was Louis' answer.

Seizing his sister's arm, he hustled her off to the railroad station. "Yep," the ticket seller replied to his question, "there's a train leaving for Chicago at ten tonight and it carries a Jim Crow car. Boy, you're in luck!"

Louis' next move was to rush home to make his preparations and tell his mother the stupendous news. Flinging his arms around her, he cried, "Dis is it, Mammy! I'm off at last to a real start in a big city band."

His mother's pride in her son was inevitably tinged with sorrow. "I know you'll do all right, boy," she said confidently, "but, oh, Louis, we'll miss you!"

Along Perdido Street and through Storyville word of Satchmo's sudden eminence had spread swiftly. A large crowd of well-wishers were at the station to bid him farewell. Pride in the New Orleans boy who had made good shone on every face. From his perch on the car step Louis looked down upon them, clowning and joking to draw attention from the tears in his eyes. He knew how these men felt. It was not only personal affection for him. An advancement for one individual inspired hope of better opportunities for all of them. The friendliness of their good-by helped him endure the long, dusty, uncomfortable journey in the dirty car reserved for colored travelers.

It was ten o'clock at night when Louis reached Chicago's La Salle Street station. At the information booth he was told to take the elevated railroad to reach Lincoln Gardens at Thirty-first Street in South Chicago. When the train came sliding along the platform, he looked anxiously for the Jim Crow car but could not see one. To his surprise and relief, he found both colored and white people seated in the car he was obliged to enter. It was weird to be whisked past the upper floors of tenements so close that he looked right into the faces of people lolling out of the windows.

After getting off at his station, he managed to find Lincoln Gardens by asking the way a number of times. It was a large, square building which he recognized at once by the electric sign. So this was King Oliver's place! He went in at the side entrance and climbed the back stairway that led to the band platform. Setting down his heavy suitcase, he gazed around with eager eyes.

By chance he had come in during an intermission. Around the piano was gathered a laughing group of men in tuxedos. Before he could identify the leader he saw a familiar face turned toward him. "Baby Dodds!" he cried. "Man, how are you?"

Dodds had been a drummer on Louis' second Mississippi trip. With a cry of welcome, he leaped between a couple of music stands to grab Louis by both arms. "Satchmo! You're here!"

All the others turned from the piano. Joe Oliver, tall and ponderous, strode across the platform. Smiling broadly, he shook Louis' hand and gave him a hearty thump on the back. "It sure is great to see you, Satchmo! That your suitcase? Good. You're comin' right home with me after we close. Take a seat down there and we'll give you an earful."

After Dodds' brother Johnny and the other players had greeted him, Louis found a seat down front. It was fascinating to listen to the band of which he was to be a part. Here, indeed, was pure, unadulterated jazz, played by experienced and gifted musicians. It was by far the most remarkable group assembled in those early days of jazz. And when Oliver stepped forward to take the lead in "High Society," he proved to the entire audience his right to bear the title *King*.

Turning in his chair, Louis studied the patrons. The roomy dance floor could accommodate about fifty couples. Other guests who were obviously there to enjoy the music sat at tables bordering the dancing space. Applause was generous after each number.

Still much too excited to feel tired, Louis was surprised when the musicians began packing up their instruments. A glance at his watch told him that it was nearly half past two! In response to Oliver's beckoning finger, he mounted the platform to congratulate the band. Then, suitcase in hand, he followed Joe to the street.

Louis' second trip on the elevated took him and his friend to a dark, dingy street lined with tenements. But the upstairs flat they entered was roomy and pleasant. Hastening from the kitchen, Mrs. Oliver cried, "Well, if it isn't Satchmo!" In a few minutes she set an enticing supper of red beans before the hungry pair. Between each mouthful Louis was kept busy answering questions about all the well-known "cats," or jazz players, in New Orleans.

The next day at rehearsal Louis discovered, to his disappointment, what his role in the band was supposed to be. Louis' cornet was merely to serve as foil for King Oliver's trumpet—to be only a part of the ensemble, not to play solos. In spite of his fondness for Papa Joe and his gratitude to him, Louis was dashed by this prospect. He found himself wondering what he could do about the situation. After a few weeks he tried an experiment.

"Say, Joe," he urged during a rest period at rehearsal, "while I was on de boat I fixed up a song for a jazz band. I even sold it to a phonograph man for a record. Wonder if we could try it."

Oliver looked interested. "Well, might be a good break. What is it, Satchmo?"

"I call it 'Sister Kate,' and folks who're crazy 'bout the shimmy like it real well." Throwing back his head, he sang the verse.

"I wish I could shimmy like my sister Kate,
  She dances like a jelly on a plate."

Oliver and the others roared with laughter. Then they gleefully began to work out the parts. Louis sang and played the song until the band had perfected it and that evening they tried it out.

Standing at one side of the players, Louis sang, played, and clowned the new number. Before long the crowd was responding with shouts of joy to the powerful tenor voice, the laughter in the big, rolling eyes, and the exaggerated movements of the flexible young body. When he finished, they clapped and stamped until he sang it again. Even as he bowed his thanks, he wondered whether Oliver would resent his success. But Joe, sensing no competition from a singer, was applauding and laughing with the rest.

Having thus established himself as an individual, Louis found it easier to give up the idea of solo performances on the cornet. He taught the band another of his compositions, which was finally called "Sugarfoot Stomp," and it became a favorite immediately.

Playing with such a band was, he knew, an excellent opportunity to increase his knowledge of the various ways of achieving the truly professional style he craved. Although the players never had individually scored parts, they did read new music. But Louis did not yet feel competent to read difficult scores and began to think about getting further instruction.

On his first day off Louis took the elevated into the heart of the city. Michigan Boulevard seemed to him the most beautiful avenue he had ever seen. Not far from it he found dark, crowded streets, tawdry lunchrooms, and shabby buildings. But even in the gloomy thoroughfares under the elevated, people tore along with cheerful zest. Policemen from whom he asked directions were friendly and store clerks were polite. Bustling Chicago did not emphasize exclusive privileges for white folks.

Once, on a free night, Louis strolled into Dreamland, a handsome cabaret not far from Lincoln Gardens. Hardly had he sat down when his eyes were caught by the band's pianist. She was a beautifully dressed, distinguished-looking young colored woman, whose playing was a marvel of skill and authority. He moved to a table near the platform in order to watch her fleet, slender hands. During a pause she lifted her head and looked straight at him. In that second he received the impression of a striking personality and a keen intelligence. He left the

cabaret wondering if he could find someone to introduce him to her.

To his astonishment, he found her at Joe Oliver's rehearsal a few days later. Joe promptly presented him to Lil Hardin, "the world's best pianist." Louis was too breathless to talk, but with a warm smile Lil drew him into conversation as if they were old friends. When she said she had been engaged as Oliver's pianist, his heart gave a thump of joy. It was daunting, however, to learn that Miss Hardin was a college graduate with a degree in music. How could he ever make friends with such a highbrow?

Lil's playing gave the band new impetus. Rehearsals were always entertaining. One afternoon, at the end of a revised version of "Choo Choo Blues," she dropped her hands and faced the band.

"Oh, boys," she cried, "there's never been anything like these jazz rhythms before. And what a marvelous glissando!"

Intently Louis considered this comment. He realized that the three-beat rhythm imposed on a basic four-beat was what had first excited him about this music. As for *glissando,* that, of course, described the swooping succession of notes played by trumpet and cornet. He was charmed to hear Lil express such opinions about the new musical creations from the South.

He wished he could say that to her, but he was awed by her accomplishments. During a rest period she often played what Louis knew was called classical music. Hanging over the piano, he listened to the beautiful melodies, convinced that Lil Hardin was the personification of romance.

Papa Joe and the other men soon began to tease Louis about his absorption in the pianist. His response was an embarrassed grin, but Lil laughed gaily at their sallies. One day, however, she showed a partiality for Louis that surprised him as much as it angered Oliver.

Rising from the piano bench after a rehearsal of "Panama," Lil said, "Papa Joe, why don't you ever give Satchmo a real chance?"

"What do you mean?" the leader snapped, with a glowering look.

"You never let him have a solo part. Why don't you give him a chance to blow the way you know he can? Let me tell you, some of the patrons here say you're afraid to."

Silent and appalled, Louis saw Joe Oliver's big bulk actually quiver with fury. "Who's afraid? I ain't afraid of nobody's blowin'. Why should I be? I'm King Oliver and everybody knows it."

Quite unperturbed by his anger, Lil replied, "Of course you're the King, Papa Joe, and you've got a

great band. But any band has to make the most of
each man's talent. Your band won't reach its high
mark unless you feature Louis. He's a draw with the
crowd."

Oliver was still glaring. "Satchmo can blow his
head off as long as he's just part of this band."

Louis could stand no more. "I'm stayin' right
with you, Papa Joe. Bein' here means everythin' to
me."

With a shrug Oliver walked away and began to
sort some music. Baby Dodds and his brother John
were grinning and nodding their approval of Lil's
plea. The rehearsal went on.

That night Louis tried to thank Lil for her cham-
pionship, but he was always tongue-tied in her pres-
ence. Between infatuation and consciousness of her
superiority, he felt choked.

At first the program went on as usual. When the
band began to play "Muskrat Ramble," however,
something new occurred. Each man was playing the
theme in his individual way, but at the same time
harmonizing his part with the whole. Oliver, of
course, was leading. Everyone was listening for the
pause or break, after which Oliver usually took up
the melody in a different key. Without a signal, by
mutual inspiration alone, Joe and Louis made the
pause and then repeated the melody in thirds. The

variation proved so effective that shouts for repetition came from the floor.

Oliver took the bows and struck up the piece again. When the King boomed into his solo part, voices from the floor called, "Armstrong! We want Armstrong!" "Let him blow!" "Come on, kid!" Even the Dodds brothers joined in. "Let him blow, Papa Joe!" With a final flourish Oliver stepped back and waved Louis to the front.

His chance at last! Behind him he felt the eager support of Lil and the band. With youthful power and daring, Louis threw himself into a really virtuoso performance. The original style of his phrasing drew roars of applause from the listeners. Panting with effort and exaltation, Louis turned to Joe Oliver, shouting, "There's the King!" But the audience would not let him stop and once more his pinnacle of sustained sound aroused a tumult.

Walking back to his place at last, Louis cast an uneasy glance at Oliver. Such an ovation for someone else must have been hard to take. Joe was smiling genially at the audience, but at closing time his manner to the members of the band was cool. Louis resolved to cajole him out of the dark mood when they went home to supper.

As he started out, however, there was a light touch on his arm. Lil, who had hardly looked at him after the solo, was there beside him. "Papa Joe," she called, "I'm kidnaping your boy to share a little snack with me. Hope you don't mind."

In surprise Oliver turned and surveyed them. "Well, good night then," he said abruptly, and walked on.

Tucking her hand into Louis' arm, Lil steered him out to the street. "Oh, Satchmo," she exclaimed, "nothing ever gave me such a thrill as your playing tonight. It was sheer magic."

As they faced each other across a table in a quiet little eating place, Lil drew Louis into talk about his life in New Orleans. Her eyes sparkled with interest and she laughed gaily at his descriptions.

Suddenly, however, she grew serious. "Louis, your talent is remarkable. Yet I knew right away that you'd had no musical background. Jazz is wonderful, but, Satchmo, think of all the music you don't know—opera, symphonies, concertos!"

"Dat's right," he agreed humbly. "I ain't even heard t'ings like dat, let alone studied 'em like you have."

She went on eagerly. "Lots of colored musicians have been successful at singing and playing classical music. Of course we're proud of them. But this new music is more important to us. We've created it. Colored artists are the only ones who can really

play it the way it should be played. I'd never want
you to give up jazz. But a gifted man like you ought
to learn something of the whole range of music."
Breaking off, she looked into his adoring eyes.
"Louis, you're sweet—not a bit conceited. I've gone
on this way because I've thought about you so much.
Would you let me teach you something about the
other kind of music? And play you some of the great
things?"

"Oh, baby!" he breathed. "Dat would be wonderful!"

She tossed back her head and glanced at him
through her long eyelashes. "Come up to my room
tomorrow afternoon and I'll play for you. Maybe

you'll blow some of my favorite arias for me."

And so a new chapter in Armstrong's life began. He spent hours beside Lil's piano listening to her play Chopin, Brahms, Bach, Scarlatti, Debussy. Whenever she could persuade him to make the effort to put his mind on it, she gave him a lesson in sight reading. Then she played him opera records on the phonograph. As soon as a record stopped whirring, Louis would pick up his cornet. His ear was so accurate and his memory so remarkable that he could repeat any aria, from Verdi to Mozart.

One day, after Lil had put on a record, she stood back to watch Louis' reaction. A full orchestra was playing W. C. Handy's "St. Louis Blues." The tone was rich. Melancholy dripped from the violins. Clarinets crooned and the brasses lifted the theme into a splendor of sound.

Louis kept nodding his head delightedly. When the record ended, he asked quickly, "What orchestra is dat?"

"Paul Whiteman's. You know—he's the first big orchestra leader to play jazz. How do you like his work?"

"I like it fine," replied Louis. "I bet Whiteman makes blues and jazz de rage. Dat's good, all right. It's good for everybody." He stopped and thought. " 'Course, though, Whiteman ain't playin' real jazz

—not de New Orleans kind. He got de music written down and fixed in certain notes and de musicians plays 'em and nothin' else. No player in an orchestra can improvise. What dey do and what King Oliver's band does is different as night from day."

"Do you think then," asked Lil, "there'll be two kinds of jazz playing?"

"Dat's it—two kinds!" said Louis eagerly. "Orchestrated, written jazz—dat some conductors'll sweeten up—and jazz played by bands of not more dan seven or eight. A good jazz band'll never play a piece exactly de same, on account of de performers bein' free to put in variations de rest will understand and follow."

Lil's eyes glowed with interest. "Yes, that's the New Orleans style. And when musicians like Oliver and Freddy Keppard and Johnny Dodds came here to Chicago, they brought that original jazz with them and Chicago became its center. I guess New York—Broadway, at least—will likely become a center for written, orchestrated jazz. You put it in a nutshell, Satchmo."

Now that Joe Oliver understood that Lil and Louis really cared for each other, he beamed upon them with fatherly affection. His joking at their expense was always kindly. Moreover, he began to give

Louis the stage several times during an evening.

Stimulated by competition with the King, Louis was improving in style week by week. His plaintive singing of the blues, which expressed the sorrow and longing of his race, was in striking contrast to the triumphant blast of sound from his cornet. Thanks to his expanded knowledge of old-world music, he often introduced themes from it into his jazz compositions. His fame was spreading fast and crowds packed Lincoln Gardens every night.

Instinctively he and Lil were testing each other. During the spring of 1923, excursions into the country, picnics on the beaches of Lake Michigan, proved their mutual love of the out-of-doors. Lil made it plain that Louis' originality, vivacity, and charm more than made up for any lack of culture on his part. As a result, his sensitiveness about that lack disappeared.

It was not long before they decided to get married and each immediately set about obtaining a divorce. When this was accomplished, they announced their plans to the Olivers one night when they were at their apartment for dinner. Papa Joe's unfeigned delight drew them all closer together.

At first the newly married couple rented a small apartment. Louis, in spite of helping his mother and sister and sending occasional sums to Daisy, was piling up savings. He had an ambitious plan of making purchases that would please his wife and draw her closer, for sometimes she seemed remote to the twenty-three-year-old youth who up to now had always lived completely in the moment.

She was right beside him, nevertheless, to help him solve the family problems that suddenly arose. First came the unexpected arrival of his mother. Delighted as he was to see her, he and Lil had to find and furnish an apartment for her. Soon afterwards a widowed cousin of Louis' died in New Orleans, leaving a subnormal boy who was incapable of taking care of himself. Urged on by Lil, Louis decided to give him a home, and his mother offered to look after the boy. The arrangement was short-lived. The old lady grew homesick for New Orleans and could not be persuaded to stay in Chicago. There was nothing for the Armstrongs to do but send her back and take the boy into their own home. Neither of them resented the obligation for a moment. With a warmth that deeply touched Louis, Lil set about finding the right training school for their charge.

The gifts Louis bought for his wife helped to make their home in Chicago seem perfect. A handsome grand piano was one of his first purchases. Then he bought a fine new house. Hardly were the Armstrongs and the little boy comfortably settled in it, however, when Joe Oliver dropped a bomb. In the midst of a rehearsal he jubilantly announced that he had received an excellent offer to take his band on tour through Ohio, Indiana, and Illinois. Of course all the boys would sign up with him, wouldn't they?

The musicians stared first at Oliver and then at one another. Oliver looked imploringly into their faces. "You surely ain't goin' back on me," he said pleadingly.

Baby Dodds was the first to speak. "I can't see it, Papa Joe. Chicago's my beat. I'm afraid you'll have to count me out."

His brother Johnny echoed him. Then, one by one, others shook their heads, made excuses, and gently but firmly refused to leave the city. Meanwhile, Louis was exchanging frantic silent messages with Lil. She nodded gravely and he turned back to Oliver, who stood there silent with incredulity and disappointment.

"Well, Papa Joe," said Louis, "Lil and I are just settled in our new house, but we'll go with you. We couldn't desert you nohow."

Oliver, in spite of his relief and gratitude, was in a frenzy of anxiety. "What are we going to do for a band?" he wailed.

Louis had an answer ready. Recently he had heard

from friends in New Orleans that a group of musicians were looking for an engagement. Oliver promptly communicated with them, and it was not long before a good band had assembled for the tour.

Strenuous weeks of travel and playing one-night stands followed. The high light of the tour for Louis was the novel experience of making records. Lil, who was greatly interested in this, predicted that the sale of his records would do much to make Louis known throughout the country.

Joe Oliver's hope that return to Chicago would mean an engagement with his new band at the old stand was short-lived, for Lincoln Gardens burned to the ground. Oliver easily found a job as trumpeter, but it was not the same as having his own group. After a few weeks Lil and Louis joined the band at Dreamland, to Lil's great delight. Once more the prospect looked calm and pleasant—and once more fate intervened. A telegram from New York arrived for Louis one afternoon.

Lil watched him tear it open and stand staring at the message. He did not hear her impatient question. His thoughts were flashing back to three years before when the same man had made him the same offer. How frightened he had been then at the idea of leaving his beloved New Orleans! How glad he was when the offer fell through! But now—

"It's from Fletcher Henderson, honey," he said, finally answering Lil's repeated questions. "He wants me to join his band at Roseland in New York City."

She was silent a moment. Then she said, "Of course you know Henderson is his own pianist. I can't be with you there."

"But you'll go East with me, Lil, till I get started? I couldn't face dat town widout you. It's mighty big!"

"Go with you?" she echoed sharply. "You mean you've decided right away to accept? Why, Louis,

do you think you're really ready for Broadway? You're unknown in New York. And you still don't read music well." Seeing the mixture of doubt and yearning in his face, she added more gently, "Of course, it's a big feather in your cap, Satchmo."

"It's come to me," he said slowly. "I turned Fletcher Henderson down once. Maybe dis is de way I gotta grow taller, Lil. Seems like I oughta go."

Springing up from her chair, Lil flung her arms around him. "All right, boy, I'll go with you and see you dive off."

A few days later, on the corner of 50th Street and Broadway, the Armstrongs stood gazing at the buildings of New York looming skyward in the purple dusk of late October.

6. *High Notes*

"There you are! Good gal!" Louis seized Lil's arm and drew her apart from the sauntering Broadway crowd.

"Well!" Lil's glance and tone brimmed with reproach. "I've been waiting on this corner for half an hour. What on earth have you been doing?"

"Oh, Lil, I've been seein' Harlem. A man told me how to go by subway. I took de wrong one and hadda come back a ways. But next time I made it. I musta walked miles. Wait till you see de wide streets, de stores an' big apartments, de dance halls an' theaters!"

Lil gave a half-amused little sniff. "I'll see it all right. Harlem's where we have to stay."

"Yep, and it's great. Say, I got to talkin' to a man in a cafeteria. He knew all de music hot shots. An' what you t'ink? My old pal Buster Bailey's around. I took a Fift' Avenue bus back down. It goes right along de big park wid millionaires' houses on one side."

She smiled at his enthusiasm. "It *is* exciting to be here, Satchmo," she replied. Then, with a start, she glanced across the street. "Look! I see bright lights at Roseland. It must be time for rehearsal. Let's go on over."

"I reckon we better," he said slowly, but he did not stir. "Lawsie, Lil, I'm scared."

She patted his arm. "Just wait till they hear you, baby. Come on now."

At the top of a wide flight of stairs the door to a huge, handsomely decorated ballroom stood open. Lil slipped into the shadows as Louis walked up to the platform. As the musicians strolled in, each one nodded at Louis. "Howdy! Guess you're the new man." Eyes fixed him with aloof curiosity. Remembering that Lil had said he was quite unknown in New York, Louis felt suddenly lost and far away from his former admiring associates. Eagerly he watched for Fletcher Henderson.

But as Louis stepped forward, smiling, Henderson merely said, "Oh, you must be Louis Armstrong. Good! You'll find your part on the stand. You're third cornet."

My part! thought Louis in terror. I gotta read it at sight?

Sure enough. There on his music rack was the third-cornet part for a piece called "Minnetonka." Never before had he faced this situation. In Fate Marable's band, where he had first learned to read a little, they did not have individual scores for the different instruments, and he could make up his own part as he went along.

Paralyzed by this unexpected demand on his musicianship, the frightened young man made only a pretense of reading his part and blowing his cornet while he listened with intense concentration. When, however, the piece was played again, he followed softly but accurately. He was really playing by ear and at the same time recognizing the notes on the score. Aware that the other bandsmen were watching him critically, he was in a dripping perspiration at the end of "Minnetonka."

That was Armstrong's nerve-wracking New York initiation. Joining Lil as the rehearsal ended, Louis hurried her down to the street. "Bunch of stuck-up cats, dey is!" he muttered.

Lil pressed his arm. "Just be patient, Satchmo. They'll soon find out how good you are."

He shook his head. "Maybe I oughtn't to have come." And to this his wife said nothing.

For what seemed a tedious number of weeks Louis steeled himself to endure with no sign of discomfort the cool indifference of the Roseland band. As long as Lil was with him, the fun they had during the day eased the strain of his work. But after she left to resume her job in Chicago, he ached with loneliness. Finally, however, life looked up. Henderson told Louis that a saxophone player had failed to keep his engagement and asked him if he knew anyone who could fill the empty place. At once Louis sent word to his old friend Buster Bailey to apply.

The meeting of the two friends at rehearsal warmed Louis' heart. Bailey seized both his hands and shook them up and down. "Oh, man!" he cried. "Yes, sir, old Satchmo! How's tricks?"

With a broad smile Louis answered, "Now dey'll be okay. T'ings'll liven up."

That very night the band played "Tiger Rag." Following behind Bailey's horn, Armstrong suddenly let go with his powerful blast, astonishing his fellow musicians and drawing applause from the dancers. The next day he wrote to Lil, "Now I'm *in* with the band."

At once he began to enjoy his work and his companions. They, in turn, responded gleefully to his gaiety. Unlike Fletcher Henderson, they considered his lack of musical education less important than his talent. One afternoon they greeted a sensational mistake of his with affectionate laughter instead of derision.

The band was trying out an intricate arrangement of Irish waltzes. After a fortissimo passage came a phrase that was merely whispered; that is, by everyone except Louis, who went roaring on all by himself. When Henderson's frantic gesture stopped him, he looked up in surprise.

"Louis," asked the conductor sharply, "are you blind? Can't you read the score marks?"

"Sure!" he answered in a slightly indignant tone.

"Is that so? Then just what do you think those double *P's* over the last passage mean?"

Louis placed his finger on the page. "Why, dey mean *pound plenty!*" he answered promptly.

The delighted howls meeting this reply drowned Henderson's anger. Under cover of the prolonged mirth, Buster Bailey leaned over to the puzzled cornetist. "That's Italian, Satchmo. *F* stands for forte, or loud. *P* means piano, or soft; and double *P* means very soft."

"Lawsie!" muttered Louis with an abashed grin. "Why can't dey use plain English?"

With chagrin, he remembered how Lil had tried to make him really work over new scores. This latest blunder inspired him to study as never before. Somewhat to his disgust, he found that Henderson, who liked to introduce melting songs and "sweet jazz" into his programs, often used such keys as E or D natural. Armstrong had hard work finding his way in this totally unfamiliar realm of conventional composition. All through the winter he worked at sight reading, and his improvement won praise from the conductor.

One evening, in an irrepressible mood, Armstrong told Henderson he would like to sing the "Basin Street Blues."

"What?" laughed the conductor. "Sing? Why, you'd be a joke."

"Try me!" urged Louis, with his infectious grin.

With skeptical indulgence, Henderson gave him permission. About midnight, to the delight of the band, Louis strode to the front of the platform and began the song. When he had finished, the applause was so spontaneous and so prolonged that from then on Henderson let Louis sing once or twice every night.

One evening young Armstrong stole the show. The band played his own composition, "Sugarfoot Stomp," and Louis' cornet took the lead. His high-climbing notes dominated the drums and as he repeated the chorus the dancers stopped to listen.

With half-closed eyes he was dreaming of the past as he floated in his world of sound.

In Harlem that afternoon the sight of ragged children playing in the dirty street and an ancient Negro driving a coal cart had carried Louis back to his boyhood. Once more he felt a twinge of mingled guilt and gladness to have escaped such miseries. The listeners thrilled to the emotional throb in his playing and Henderson, crashing out the accompaniment, stared at him wonderingly.

As the break in the rhythm came, Louis lowered his cornet. There was a tense moment of waiting. Through the hush he suddenly shouted, "Oh, play that thing!"

So compelling was the emotional force of that out-cry that it was echoed by the audience. Henderson sprang to his feet to snatch both of Louis' hands. Evidently the genuine emotion in Armstrong's singing and playing of the song was talked of on Broadway, for several band leaders and soloists began to drop in at Roseland to hear him.

Other experiences brightened the laborious days of study, practice, and performance. Louis was invited once or twice to play at a late hour in the most popular Harlem cabaret, where he was warmly acclaimed.

Many celebrated colored artists gathered in Harlem that year. James Weldon Johnson was becoming well known as a poet. Florence Mills, the gifted dancer, was back from France. Ethel Waters, who greeted Louis as her friend from New Orleans, introduced him to Paul Robeson. Not yet an acknowledged Communist, Robeson was in the heyday of his distinguished career. At late parties Louis saw the noted actor, Charles Gilpin, and handsome Duke Ellington, composer and band leader. Such contacts were inspiring.

In his free daytime hours Louis was "borrowed" to make records for Clarence Williams. Williams, a music publisher, Broadway producer, and record broker, appreciated Armstrong's refusal to tamper with the fluent, vigorous style originated in New Orleans. Like the critics seriously interested in this style, Williams scorned the adulterated jazz emerging from Tin-pan Alley—the name given to the Broadway district where commercial song writers gathered. The mounting popularity of jazz inspired these pirates to swoop down on themes worked out in the deep South and glibly rearrange them for quick sale. Connoisseurs knew these productions were imitations of the real thing. It was Armstrong's high standard of performance, his extemporaneous variations, and vital swing that made his records so much in demand. His recording work was adding greatly to his reputation as well as to his income.

The winter passed swiftly. Louis was suddenly surprised to find slush vanished from the streets and forsythia flinging its gold sprays along the driveways of Central Park.

Without hesitation he signed a contract with Henderson to tour the East with the band that spring and summer. On the road he perfected a style of showmanship all his own, which made him a featured player.

The band left New York in April and opened its season in Massachusetts. New England was interesting to the young man from New Orleans. The efforts on behalf of human freedom that had been made there naturally influenced him in its favor. The quaint old taverns, white steepled churches, and spacious houses set in riotously blooming gardens represented a civilization very different from that of the Mississippi delta country. But even the huge and enthusiastic audiences in New England seemed conservative to Louis compared with the fanatic devotees of jazz in the mining towns of Pennsylvania, where the tour ended.

Fletcher Henderson expected Armstrong to stay on for another season in New York, but in spite of his gratitude for all he had learned there, Louis decided to return to Chicago. Lil had been writing him urgent letters and, in truth, he was homesick for her, for his pleasant house, his friends, and the breezy spaces of Chicago. Besides, although his horizons had widened that year and his technique had become far more professional, he was longing to take part in true jazz once more instead of the strange blend of musical styles favored by Henderson.

Henderson gave Louis a farewell banquet. In a glowing speech of praise he declared it would be impossible to replace such a gifted cornetist and good companion. Though he had been deeply touched by this testimonial, Louis boarded the train for Chicago next morning with a happy sense of release.

Lil's radiant face greeted him on the platform.

It was good to be at home again, good to relax in their cozy little house for a few days. His pleasure in the familiar Chicago scenes and in his visits with Joe Oliver and other friends, however, was dampened by Lil's insistence that he must try at once to find work. Sharply she contradicted his assumption that he would be offered an engagement without any effort on his part. Unfortunately, she was right. There was no opening for him anywhere. His enforced idleness led to constant irritability between him and his wife. When she played a Beethoven sonata, he rattled his newspaper or shook dice. When he came home late from an evening with his friends, he often found Lil in a state of fury.

"Aren't you ever going to grow up, Satchmo?" she asked one day. "You're getting fat from eating too much and you do nothing but fool away your time. You might at least read a book!"

He tried to counter with a funny story about a Harlem musician who also was out of a job, but Lil interrupted him. "Honestly, Satchmo! When are you going to give up that Perdido Street dialect? You can talk just as good English as anyone else if you feel like it! Why do you talk as if you were in a minstrel show?"

"Why, for fun!" he said, with the look of a hurt child. Then his pent-up resentment burst out. "Lil, you is de nagginest woman! You know I'm tryin' my best to land a job. Why don't you give me a break?"

Eventually that was just what she did. Learning that the cornetist at Dreamland, where she played the piano, was leaving, she recommended Louis to the manager and he was promptly engaged. Moreover, 1926 had hardly begun when a dazzling offer came from the conductor of a highly trained band playing at the Vendome, a motion-picture theater. Louis was to have a better salary than he had ever received.

"You can keep your cabaret job, too, Armstrong," said the conductor. "We close at twelve and you can skip right along to Dreamland."

Only loyalty to Lil kept Louis from accepting the offer at once. He felt it only fair to get her opinion first. When she gave her approval, he hurried to clinch his new engagement. After this decision there followed another, of great importance to his future. At the suggestion of the band leader, Louis changed from cornet to trumpet.

Paying no heed to Lil's doubts, he declared, "De trumpet is deeper and richer dan de cornet and I can climb jest as high on it. Sounds real pretty. I'm goin' to be a trumpeter from now on."

Lil made no effort to hide her boredom, her contempt of his uncultured ways, even her anger. Minor disagreements flared into stormy quarrels. Louis thought incredulously of their autumn outings on the beach, when Lil had been happy with him. To escape her tongue-lashings, he spent more and more time with friends who liked him just as he was.

Now and then the chasm between Louis and his wife was bridged by their mutual interest in jazz. She was proud when for the first time she saw her husband's name blazoned outside the theater. To his gleeful "I can hardly believe it's me in dose 'lectric lights!" she replied, "I always knew you'd make a big name, Satchmo, and I always urged you on."

She joined the group of musicians he organized at this time to make jazz recordings. The "Hot Five," as it was called, included Baby Dodds and Kid Ory, Louis' old friend from New Orleans. So well did the players know one another's style and so skillfully did they blend their individual improvisations that they hardly ever spoiled a record. Often one of the group would devise a novel arrangement of a popular song or compose something new. A recording of one of these novelties reached a sale of forty thousand in six weeks. Blues records that Louis made with well-known Negro women singers in Chicago sold astonishingly well for years and are cherished by collectors to this day.

During the wild twenties, when stocks were booming and the general American ideal seemed to be to
have a good time, Chicago became the nation's jazz
center. All schools of technique were represented.
Whiteman's orchestra and Duke Ellington's band
demonstrated the more elegant version. Most of the
famous individual drummers, pianists, and horn
players started their careers in Chicago. Armstrong,
who knew them all, had no trouble holding his own.
When a new and dynamic manager took over the
Sunset Cabaret, he persuaded Louis to leave Dreamland and organize a band for Sunset. From then on
the Armstrong name flashed on two electric signs.

Parallel with the progress in Louis' career went
the deterioration of his marriage. There seemed to
be no cure for temperamental differences, and Louis
finally applied for a divorce.

Nevertheless, when he suddenly learned that his
mother was seriously ill, he took the news straight
to Lil. Stammering in his embarrassment, he asked
her if she would go to New Orleans and bring the
old lady to Chicago. Without an instant's hesitation
Lil agreed to do it. Her warm understanding of
Louis' feeling for his mother was stronger than her
bitterness. On the trip back to Chicago with the
mortally sick woman, Lil never mentioned the break
with Louis and later, at the hospital, she joined him

in playing the role of a happy couple for his mother's benefit. Louis visited the hospital every day. In spite of the doctor's frank warning that no recovery was possible, he was profoundly shocked by his mother's death.

After the funeral he remained for several days shut away alone with his sorrow. It was an effort to return to work and the first time he faced an audience, he felt quite unequal to the demand for gaiety. The sympathetic pianist said gently, "Satchmo, how about giving them 'St. James Infirmary'?"

That was in tune with Louis' mood and, after a moment's hesitation, he nodded. The rich tones of his trumpet and his singing of the nostalgic blues song touched the listeners. With a mighty effort he finished the last verse, then fled from the platform to sob his heart out in the dressing room.

The loss of his mother ushered in a two-year period of many disappointments and anxieties for Louis. After his contract with Sunset expired, he was often out of engagements. He tried to establish a band of his own, but the project was a costly failure. Sometimes he fell so low as to play at one-night stands. For a short period he was soloist with a good band at a glamorous cabaret called the Savoy. Then the engagement ended and he and the other band members faced disaster.

Louis did not have to face it long, however. A telegram from New York brought him the offer of a job as featured player in the orchestra of a musical comedy. But even as he read the welcome message, he shook his head. What about the other members of the band?

He called them together and read the telegram aloud. As the hope in their eyes was replaced by gloom and resentment, he chuckled. "Boys," he said, "you t'ink I'd leave you in de lurch, do you? I ain't never goin' to do dat. Listen, you-all. We're goin' to New York in a bunch and bust our way into dat ol' town."

In his palmy days Louis had bought an expensive automobile. Three of the other men had cars of sorts. Gleefully they decided to pile instruments and luggage into them and drive to New York to seek their fortune.

To cover expenses on the way east, they played to delighted audiences all through Indiana, Ohio, and western New York. And at the end of their journey they won the gamble with fate. Louis not only secured his job at the theater, with his name in electric lights, he also succeeded in placing his men at Connie's Inn, a famous Harlem cabaret. He arranged this by agreeing to have them advertised, also in electric lights, as "Louis Armstrong's Band."

Early in the evening and after the theater until the small hours, Louis played with his band. In addition, he made appearances at two other Harlem cabarets.

One night at Connie's Inn he was told that a number of Broadway composers and musicians were in the audience. After his first number the group came up to the platform. Amid loud applause their spokesman presented a fine watch to Armstrong as "the man who has revolutionized jazz." This acknowledgment of indebtedness from Tin-pan Alley was an overwhelming tribute.

Besides his regular engagements, Louis was a featured player in several Broadway musicals and made a great number of records. For six months he rode the crest of the wave. When it receded, New York became just a place where gifted horn players were stranded. Louis, however, was used now to the ups and downs of his profession. He went straight to California. There, during most of 1930, he enjoyed a notable success in cabarets and recording studios. Such songs as "You're Drivin' Me Crazy," "Memories of You," and "Sleepy Time Down South" carried his ringing notes all over the country and across the seas.

A new agent signed him for winter engagements in Chicago, which were triumphantly successful. But far more exciting to the boy Louis had never ceased to be, was a summons to New Orleans. After nine years of absence, he tingled with eagerness to visit the scenes of his youth and meet the friends he had never forgotten.

When the engine whistled loudly at the outskirts of the Crescent City, Louis thrust his head out of the car window, his heart thumping with excitement. As the train crawled into the old station, he heard loud strains of jazz and in another instant beheld no fewer than eight bands lined up on the platform to blare out a welcome. From the car step two strong men snatched him up and bore him aloft on their shoulders through the madly cheering mass of people packing the streets around the station. Waving, smiling, mopping sweat and tears from his face, Louis was at last set down at the foot of Canal Street.

Then a woman rushed from the crowd, shrieking his name. It was Mamma Lucy, crying and laughing simultaneously as her brother's arms were thrown around her. It was a necessarily short greeting, for an automobile was waiting for Louis to head a jubilant procession.

White people, colored people, old friends and new, were lining the thoroughfare. A snowstorm of handkerchiefs fluttered in the hot summer air. The

cheering never ceased. Jazz players whom Louis
knew well, cabaret managers, and mere acquaint-
ances made their way through the shouting throng
to snatch his hand with a "Hi, Louis!" or "Welcome
home, Satchmo!"

Suddenly at the front of the crowd he saw Mr.
Peter Davis, his first music teacher. Behind him in
the familiar uniform were lined a dozen boys holding up a banner bearing the name *Colored Waifs'
Home Band.* Telling the driver to stop the car,

Louis leaned over and called, "Hello, Mr. Davis! It's great to see you!"

The man who had once so terrified young Armstrong shook the hand held out to him with warm friendliness. Then he turned to the youngsters. "Boys, you know about Louis Armstrong, the famous trumpeter. We're all mighty proud of him at the Home, aren't we?"

When Louis promised to go out to see them, their grateful shouts seemed to Louis the climax of his exciting progress up Canal Street.

That evening Perdido Street claimed its own. Strung across it was a banner announcing Louis Armstrong's return. In the cabarets the bands were playing his famous arrangements of "Sugarfoot Stomp" and "Sister Kate." At every step he was so surrounded by admirers that his wrist ached from shaking hands and his cheek muscles grew stiff from smiling.

But the answers to his eager inquiries about boys he had once known well saddened him. Some were dead, some in jail, several had had to flee from justice—nobody knew where. Many were the hard-luck stories of young men hit by the depression. It flashed on Armstrong's consciousness that the contrast between such misfortunes and his own successful career was the chief reason for the extravagant celebration over his return. He represented pride and hope to Perdido Street folk.

The very next morning Louis drove out to the Colored Waifs' Home. As he shook hands with Mr. and Mrs. David Jones, he said gaily, "Know what? It's just seventeen and a half years since de day I was brought here for shootin' dat gun."

Peter Davis seized his arm. "Come, Louis! The band is ready and the boys are all waiting for you."

Louis crossed the threshold of the big room to a round of applause. Acknowledging it with his wide smile, he cried, "Go ahead and play, kids! I'm listenin'!" At the end of "A Hot Time in the Old Town Tonight," he clapped loudly. Then he walked up to the platform and held out his hand to the boy who had been blowing his old cornet. "Let me see it!" he said. Stroking the worn instrument lovingly, he put it to his lips and played "Basin Street Blues" for the excited youngsters.

Louis skipped nothing. He looked at the playground and into the classrooms where he had received a little learning and a great many whacks. Up in the dormitory he went straight to his old bed and stretched out on it with a grateful sigh. As he left, the boys jammed the hall to bid him good-by. By this time they knew that their guest had brought them many gifts—a phonograph with a pile of rec-

ords, big boxes of candy, and for every member of
the band a fine linen handkerchief like his own.

"I've been grateful all dese years for bein' sent to
dis school," he said, "and before I leave town I'm
goin' to hunt up ol' Judge Wilson and tell him so."

In the end he kept his promise. But before that
night was over, he was far from certain he could do
so. There was a moment, indeed, when he believed
he could hardly leave New Orleans quickly enough.

Louis had been engaged to play as soloist with a
band at Suburban Gardens. When he and his agent
drove out there, they found a large portion of the
city's colored population massed outside the en-
closure. Although they were not allowed to come
in, they were obviously hoping to hear the famous
trumpet. The size of the crowd milling about
seemed to alarm the police, who were struggling to
keep the people back and subdue their clamor. The
sight aroused in Louis that shuddering apprehension
of trouble so close to the surface among colored citizens in the South.

Inside, the manager greeted Louis cordially. "We
have a record crowd tonight, Armstrong," he said.
"There must be five thousand people waiting to
hear you."

Louis managed to smile, but the news only in-
creased his uneasiness. In what mood had these

white folk come? He was suddenly unsure of his reception in this southern city. As he went on the stage, shrouded from view of the audience by heavy curtains, the men in the band greeted him with wide grins.

"All set to open with 'Sleepy Time Down South'?" he asked in a low tone.

"Ready, Satchmo," whispered the band leader, "soon as the M.C. gives his spiel over the microphone."

In silence they all watched the blond master of ceremonies, elegant in evening clothes, stride past them. He slid between the curtains, which closed behind him. There was a brief burst of applause. Then, evidently at the microphone, he began in his suave voice, "Ladies and gentlemen, we have with us tonight—" The voice ceased. There was a pause. Electric tension throbbed from the unseen audience to the waiting musicians. Then the ominous silence was broken. The master of ceremonies shouted, "I'm not— I just *can't* introduce this nigger!"

Instantly a pandemonium of shouts, boos, catcalls, and stamping broke out. From the wings the manager rushed out to confront the appalled members of the band. "What does it mean? Is it a riot? I don't know what to do!"

Louis faced him sternly. "I'll take dis on!" he said.

Slipping between the curtain folds, he stepped out into the glare of footlights and spotlights. He could see nothing. The explosion of sound that met his appearance struck terror into his very bones. What was going to happen?

All at once he discovered that he was hearing a hailstorm of clapping and repeated shouts of his name. It was a tremendous welcome. They were friends out there! His relief was so great that his knees shook. Mopping his brow and forcing a smile to his lips, he said hoarsely, "Thank you, folks, thanks one and all!"

The curtains were parting. The band sounded the first bars of "Sleepy Time Down South." Louis lifted his trumpet and the concert began. All the fear and joy he had just experienced poured into his playing, reaching a climax in his clear and powerful high C sharp. Another ovation followed and Louis had to take several bows before he could let his trembling body sink into a chair behind the piano.

All evening the enthusiasm kept up. The exultant manager assured Louis that he had fired the outrageous master of ceremonies on the spot. During the drive back to the hotel with his agent, Armstrong learned that the evening's success had won him a contract to play at Suburban Gardens for four months.

It was a happy period. To hold the interest of large audiences consistently Louis had to work hard. In his free hours he could roam the city in a dreamy review of the past. He had wanted to visit the slum where he was born, but he found that the ramshackle houses had been torn down. He haunted the levees where he and his friends used to sing in the moonlight. He swam in Lake Pontchartrain and visited his old grandmother. And everywhere he went he filled his nostrils with the fragrance of honeysuckle and roses.

Unfortunately, an incident at the end of his stay cast a shadow upon it. For weeks Louis had been trying in vain to give a big free performance for the colored citizens of New Orleans. Somehow, difficulties always arose. Finally, however, arrangements were made for a mammoth concert at the Army Base. Then, at the last moment, when hundreds of people were gathered before the door and Louis was on his way, permission to use the Base was withdrawn with no warning whatsoever. The police had no explanation to give the disappointed crowd. Louis could never bear to speak of this cruel treatment of his powerless people.

During the autumn Armstrong went first to California and then to Chicago for engagements. He was a rich man now. Never again was he obliged to face financial worries or wait anxiously for an opening in a band. In 1932 he mounted to a new high level when his manager arranged a tour of Great Britain.

Louis heard this news with trepidation. He felt no assurance that he was known abroad or that any appreciation of jazz existed in the British Isles. Yet his faith in the future allowed him to feel a thrill of excitement as he walked up the gangplank of the *Majestic*. Not long after sailing, he received a cable from England's leading trumpet player, promising that he would meet Louis at Plymouth. The British trumpeter was there not only to greet the visitor but to report that a banquet in his honor was being given that night in London.

In this cordial fashion Armstrong's English experience began. It was a glad surprise to discover how well his name was known, how many thousands of young people had been playing his records. During his two weeks' engagement at a London theater the house was packed to the doors every night and no British reserve checked the response of the audience. True, the classicists among the music critics were haughty about both the trumpeter and his programs, but more liberal reviewers praised Armstrong's amazing technique and hotly defended the importance of jazz. With golden guineas tumbling into his pocket and autograph collectors besieging him after every performance, Louis could afford to ignore journalistic snubs.

"What gives me a big surprise," he said to a new-found friend, "is how a lot of you seem to respect jazz over here. It gets boosted right up wid operas and symphonies by your highbrow writers. Dat's a rare t'ing in my country so far."

For his scheduled concerts throughout England and Scotland, Armstrong summoned a number of jazz musicians from Paris to fill out his band. He spent hours every day rehearsing with them for the tour, which turned out to be an outstanding success.

It was with a sense of farewell to friends that Louis stood before the monster gathering in the Music Hall for his last performance. Each number he played seemed to produce more and more tumultuous applause. Toward the end of the program a voice like a megaphone shouted, "Play 'Tiger Rag,' Louis!" and the request was loudly repeated from every corner of the hall.

Armstrong had not offered this piece before, because he thought it was too dated to be known in England. Delighted to grant the request, he bowed and waved his trumpet with a wide smile of appreciation.

The instant he joined the band in the old tune a curious fantasy took possession of him. He was no longer a man in well-pressed evening clothes facing a vast audience in London. He was a ragged, barefoot urchin in New Orleans, singing this tune to his first listeners—the riffraff of Perdido Street. He could see faces leaning from windows, hear the raucous laughter of drunken sailors stopping to listen. Even a nervous expectation of police interference made his scalp prick. Could all this have happened nearly twenty years ago? Now the same dusty little urchin was being acclaimed in one of the great capitals of the world as an artist of renown. "Tiger Rag"! The strains he was playing to spellbound Britishers seemed to signify his progress through adolescence to manhood, from frustration to triumph.

Something of this emotional review must have colored his playing. When at last he lowered his trumpet from quivering lips, wave after wave of applause and cheers thundered through the hall. "A mass demonstration of incredible proportions," declared the morning journals.

By the time Armstrong returned to the United States he had become a cosmopolitan, ready to meet

distinguished people with complete ease. Since that time he has traveled widely all over Europe and even to Japan. Concerts before royalty hold no terrors for him. Once when George V of England sat in a box at one of Armstrong's performances, he was convulsed with laughter when Louis, with a low bow, turned and sang, directly to him, a famous blues song, "You Rascal, You!"

Louis was at last lucky enough to win a charming wife who combines unfailing devotion with great personal dignity. His impetuous and ceaseless generosity, which make it difficult for her to save much from his large earnings, is her only cause for worry. Unlike Lil, who is a warm friend of the Armstrongs, unlike many more conventional colored people, Lucille Armstrong thoroughly enjoys her husband's public drolleries. She knows they are part of his showmanship and quite disassociated from his art.

Lucille, who is considerably younger than Louis, finds nothing surprising in the present widespread critical appreciation of her husband's work as a jazz artist. Typical of such praise is the published comment by the composer and critic, Virgil Thomson: "His style of improvisation would seem to have combined the highest reaches of instrumental virtuosity with the most tensely disciplined melodic structure and the most spontaneous emotional expression, all of which in one man you must admit is pretty rare."

Interviewed once about the essentials of his art, Louis said, "Hard work and precision and skill are no more than enough for real playing. I don't like the sloppy way some trumpeters have of wavin' around a note. Every time *F* is supposed to be hit—mop! There it is! It's gotta be that way. You gotta have the repertoire and the ingredients to make music."

King Louis, as one noted critic has called him, wears his crown like a beret, for he has no illusions of grandeur. His is a success story, but he never forgets that it began in the sordid poverty of Perdido Street. He remembers that fame came slowly and he cherishes the many individuals who helped him achieve it. His rare talent, supported by unflagging work, maintains his position, year after year, as America's greatest trumpeter. It is, however, his gay and incorruptible naturalness that continues to win for Louis Armstrong a world-wide affection.

JEANETTE EATON was born in Columbus, Ohio, and was brought up in a household where books and music, friends and a garden were enjoyed and valued. She was graduated from Vassar College and received her master's degree from Ohio State University. After trying different jobs in various parts of the United States, she wrote stories and articles for magazines and newspapers before settling down to write books for young people, a field to which she now devotes herself almost entirely. "Biography for young people is my vocation," she says. "It is a choice one, which permits constant association with the great people of this earth." In her many fine biographies, Miss Eaton has made it possible for her readers to enjoy the same wonderfully good company. She writes about people who are not only famous but extremely interesting, and she tells their stories with contagious enthusiasm.